KANT AND SPENCER

A STUDY OF THE

FALLACIES OF AGNOSTICISM

DR. PAUL CARUS

Wipf and Stock Publishers
EUGENE, OREGON

Wipf and Stock Publishers
199 West 8th Avenue, Suite 3
Eugene, Oregon 97401

Kant and Spencer
A Study of the Fallacies of Agnosticism
By Carus, Paul
ISBN: 1-59244-237-4
Publication date 5/9/2003
Previously published by The Open Court Publishing Company

PREFACE.

MODERN philosophy begins with Kant because Kant broke with the traditional Dogmatism and supplanted it by Criticism. He proposed the new plan of building doctrines upon the firm ground of experience. Kant was the first positivist in the sense that all philosophy must be based upon facts. How strange that in France and England his views were misunderstood by those who endeavored to progress along the same lines! Auguste Comte denounced Kant as an antiquated metaphysician and Herbert Spencer looks upon him as the champion of mediævalism and dogmatism. The truth is that neither the former nor the latter knew anything of Kant and so wasted their powder without demolishing their enemy but they did a great deal of harm by leading the public astray and perverting the real issues. They themselves failed in their main aspirations; neither Comte nor Spencer succeeded in proposing a scientific philosophy; both ended in agnosticism, which is practically a declaration of philosophical bankruptcy.*

The merits of both Comte and Spencer cannot be underrated; both did good work in collecting and systematising material,—the former, a mathematical genius, in a truly scientific manner, the latter as a populariser. Comte became better acquainted with Kant in his advanced age and regretted deeply that he had misunderstood the trend of his thought, because he thus missed the benefit of his wholesome influence.

I do not say that it is necessary to be a Kantist in any sense; but to be a leader of thought, a leader that leads onward and forward, it is indispensable to understand Kant. Mr. Spencer's attitude toward Kant has remained disdainful and even hostile. This

* For a discussion of French positivism as represented by Auguste Comte and his most illustrious disciple Emile Littré see *Monist*, Vol. II, pp. 403-417

is the more to be regretted as Mr. Spencer possesses many rare accomplishments that would naturally have fitted him to become an apostle of progress. He is regarded so by many of his adherents and enemies, but only by those who are superficially acquainted with philosophical problems. I do not hesitate to say that Mr. Spencer is a reactionary spirit. He seems progressive because he objects to the religious dogmas that have been established by tradition, but he is reactionary because he boldly sets up nescience as a philosophical principle, and the time is near at hand when his very enemies will take refuge in his doctrines.

We have a high respect for Mr. Spencer as a man and a thinker, but it is a great pity that with all his brilliant talents, with all his ambition and energy, he has been deficient in thoroughness and earnestness. As a philosopher, he is a dilettante. Dilettantism is a marked feature not only of his entire system but also of the way in which he has worked it out. Kant was too heavy reading for him and the labor of studying his works did not seem promising. Mr. Spencer, as a thinker, follows the principle of Hedonism; he shirks the toil of research and engages in such subjects only as can easily be woven into feuilletonistic essays.

For those who think that this opinion is too severe, the articles on *Kant and Spencer*, including a discussion of *Spencerian Agnosticism*, all of which appeared some time ago in *The Open Court* and *The Monist*, are here republished in book form. The present little volume contains also Mr. Spencer's reply in full and his letter in which he declines further to enter into the subject.

In fine we have to add that these articles are not purely controversial. While they are a criticism of Mr. Spencer's flagrant mistakes they are intended to serve the higher purpose of promoting the comprehension of philosophy. They are a contribution to the history of philosophy; but the historical and literary questions here treated are after all merely the background upon which problems of basic significance are elucidated.

LA SALLE, ILL., U. S. A. THE AUTHOR.

CONTENTS.

THE ETHICS OF KANT.

MR. Herbert Spencer published in *The Popular Science Monthly* for August 1888 an essay on the Ethics of Kant; a translation of this article previously appeared in the *Revue Philosophique*, and it cannot fail to have been widely noticed. It is to be regretted that unfamiliarity with the German language and perhaps also with Kant's terminology has led Mr. Spencer into errors to which attention is called in the following discussion.*

Mr. Spencer says:

"If, before Kant uttered his often-quoted saying in which, "with the stars of Heaven he coupled the conscience of Man, as "being the two things that excited his awe, he had known more of "Man than he did, he would probably have expressed himself "somewhat otherwise."

Kant, in his famous dictum that two things excited his admiration, the starry heaven above him and the conscience within him, contrasted two kinds of sublimity.† The grandeur of the Universe is that of size and extension, while the conscience of man commands respect for its moral dignity. The universe is wonderful in its expanse and in its order of mechanical

* Quotations from Mr. Spencer's essay will be distinguished by quotation-marks, while those from Kant will appear in hanging indentations.

† Kant distinguishes two kinds of sublimity: (1) the mathematical, and (2) the dynamical. His definitions are: (1) sublime is that in comparison with which everything else is small; and (2) sublime is that the mere ability to conceive which shows a power of emotion (Gemüth), the latter transcending any measurement by the senses.—[(1) Erhaben ist, mit welchem im Vergleich alles andere klein ist. (2) Erhaben ist, was auch nur denken zu können ein Vermögen des Gemüths beweist, das jeden Maasstab der Sinne übertrifft. Editio Hartenstein, Vol. V., pp. 257, 258.]

regularity; the conscience of man is grand, being intelligent volition that aspires to be in harmony with universal laws.

Mr. Spencer continues:

"Not, indeed, that the conscience of Man is not wonderful "enough, whatever be its supposed genesis; but the wonderfulness "of it is of a different kind according as we assume it to have been "supernaturally given or infer that it has been naturally evolved. "The knowledge of Man in that large sense which Anthropology "expresses, had made, in Kant's day, but small advances. The "books of travel were relatively few, and the facts which they con- "tained concerning the human mind as existing in different races, "had not been gathered together and generalized. In our days, the "conscience of Man as inductively known has none of that univer- "sality of presence and unity of nature which Kant's saying tacitly "assumes."

Mr. Spencer apparently supposes that Kant believed in a supernatural origin of the human conscience. This, however, is erroneous.

Mr. Spencer's error is excusable in consideration of the fact that some disciples of Kant have fallen into a similar error. Professor Adler, of New York, who attempts in the Societies for Ethical Culture to carry into effect the ethics of Pure Reason, maintains that the commandments of the *ought* and "the light that shines through them come from beyond, but its beams are broken as they pass through our terrestrial medium, and the full light in all its glory we can never see."

Ethics based on an unknowable power, is mysticism; and mysticism does not essentially differ from dualism and supernaturalism.

Kant's reasoning is far from mysticism and from supernaturalism. He was fully convinced that civilized man with his moral and intellectual abilities had naturally evolved from the lower state of an animal existence. We read in his essay, "Presumable Origin of the History of Mankind" (Muthmasslicher Anfang der Menschengeschichte. Editio Hartenstein, Vol. IV, p. 321):

"From this conception of the primitive history of mankind it follows that the departure of man from the paradise represented to him by his reason as the earliest place of sojourn of his race, has been nothing else than the transition from the rude condition of a purely animal existence to the condition of a human being; a transition from the leading-strings of instinct to direction by reason, in a word, from the protectorate of nature to a status of freedom."

The view that the conscience of man is innate, in the sense of a non-natural, of a mysterious, or even of a supernatural origin, is untenable. Those disciples of Kant who entertain such views have certainly misinterpreted their great master, and the passages adduced by Mr. Spencer from so many sources are sufficient evidence of the fact that "there are widely different degrees" [we should rather say kinds] "of conscience in the different races." Mr. Spencer continues:

"Had Kant had these and kindred facts before him, his con-"ception of the human mind, and consequently his ethical con-"ception, would scarcely have been what they were. Believing, "as he did, that one object of his awe—the stellar Universe—has "been evolved,* he might by evidence like the foregoing have "been led to suspect that the other object of his awe—the human "conscience—has been evolved; and has consequently a real "nature unlike its apparent nature." * * * "If, instead of assuming "that conscience is simple because it seems simple to careless in-"trospection he had entertained the hypothesis that it is per-"haps complex—a consolidated product of multitudinous expe-"riences received mainly by ancestors and added to by self—"he might have arrived at a consistent system of Ethics." * * *

* The stellar Universe, of course, has not been evolved; Mr. Spencer means that according to Kant's mechanical explanation the planetary systems and milky ways of the stellar Universe are in a state of constant evolution.

"In brief, as already implied, had Kant, instead of his incon-"gruous beliefs that the celestial bodies have had an evolutionary "origin, but that the minds of living beings on them, or at least on "one of them, have had a non-evolutionary origin, entertained the "belief that both have arisen by Evolution, he would have been "saved from the impossibilities of his Metaphysics, and the untena-"bilities of his Ethics."

Mr. Spencer believes that Kant had assumed conscience to be "simple, because it seems simple to careless introspection." But there is no evidence in Kant's works for this assumption. On the contrary, Kant reversed the old view of so-called "rational psychology" which considered conscience as innate and which was based on the error that consciousness is simple. Des Cartes's syllogism *cogito ergo sum* is based on this idea, which at the same time served as a philosophical evidence for the indestructibility and immortality of the *ego*. The simplicity of consciousness had been considered as an axiom, until Kant came and showed that it was a fallacy, a paralogism of pure reason. Dr. Noah Porter has written, from an apparently dualistic standpoint, a sketch entitled "The Ethics of Kant," in which he says:

"The skepticism and denials of Kant's speculative theory in respect to noumena, both material and psychical, had unfortunately cut him off from the possibility of recognizing the personal *ego* as anything more than a logical fiction."

Kant says in his "Critique of Pure Reason": *

"In the internal intuition there is nothing permanent, for the *Ego* is but the consciousness of my thought. * * * From all this it is evident that rational psychology has its origin in a mere misunderstanding. The unity of consciousness, which lies at the basis of the categories, is considered to be an intuition of the subject as an object; and the category of substance is applied to the intuition. But this unity is nothing more than

* Translation by J. M. D. Meiklejohn, pp. 244, 249.

the unity in *thought*, by which no object is given; to which therefore the category of substance cannot be applied."*

Concerning the statement that Kant had believed in the non-evolutionary origin of living beings, we quote from his essay on *The Different Races of Men*, Chap. III, where Kant speaks of "the immediate causes of the origin of these different races." He says:

"The conditions (*Gründe*) which, inhering in the constitution of an organic body, determine a certain evolutionary process (*Auswickelung*†) are called, if this process is concerned with particular parts, *germs*; if, on the other hand, it touches only the size or the relation of the parts to one another, I call it *natural capabilities* (*natürliche Anlagen*)."‡

And in a foot-note Kant makes the following remark:

"Ordinarily we accept the terms natural science (*Naturbeschreibung*) and natural history in one and the same sense. But it is evident that the knowledge of natural phenomena, as they *now are*, always leaves to be desired the knowledge of that which they *have been* before now and through what succession of modifications they have passed in order to have arrived, in every respect, to their present state. *Natural History*, which at present we almost entirely lack, would teach us the changes that have affected the form of the earth, likewise, the changes in the creatures of the earth (plants and animals), that they have suffered by natural transformations and, arising therefrom, the departures from the prototype of the original species, that they have experienced. It would probably trace a great number of apparently different varieties back to species of one and the same kind and would

* Compare also Kant's "Prol. zu jeder künftigen Metaphysik," § 46.

† We call attention to Kant's peculiar expression, in this passage, of *Auswickelung* which has now yielded to the term *Entwickelung*.

‡ Die in der Natur eines organischen Körpers (Gewächses oder Thieres) liegenden Gründe einer bestimmten Auswickelung heissen, wenn diese Auswickelung besondere Theile betrifft, *Keime*; betrifft sie aber nur die Grösse oder das Verhältniss der Theile unter einander, so nenne ich sie *natürliche Anlagen*.

convert the present so intricate school-system of Natural Science into a natural system in conformity with reason." *

Kant has nowhere, so far as we know, made any objection to the idea of evolution. But he opposed the theory that all life should have originated from *one single* kind. In reviewing and epitomizing Joh. Gottfr. Herder's work, "*Ideen zur Geschichte der Menschheit*," Kant says:

* * * "Book II, treats of organized matter on the earth. * * * The beginnings of vegetation. * * * The changes suffered by man and beast through climatic influences. * * * In them all we find one prevailing form and a similar osseous structure. * * * These transitional links render it not at all impossible that in marine animals, in plants, and, indeed, possibly in so-called inanimate substances, one and the same fundamental principle of organization may prevail, although infinitely cruder and more complex in operation. In the sight of eternal being, which beholds all things in one connection, it is possible that the structure of the ice-particle, while receiving form, and of the snowflake, while being crystallized, bears an analogous relation to the formation of the embryo in a mother's womb. * * * The third book compares the structure of animals and plants with the organization of man. * * * It was not because man was ordained to be a rational creature that upright stature was given him for using his limbs according to reason; on the contrary he acquired his reason as a consequence of his upright stature. * * * From stone to crystals, from crystals to metals, from metals

* Wir nehmen die Benennungen *Naturbeschreibung* und *Naturgeschichte* gemeiniglich in einerlei Sinne. Allein es ist klar, dass die Kenntniss der Naturdinge, wie sie *jetzt sind*, immer noch die Erkenntniss von demjenigen wünschen lasse, was sie ehedem *gewesen* sind und durch welche Reihe von Veränderungen sie durchgegangen, um an jedem Ort in ihren gegenwärtigen Zustand zu gelangen. Die *Naturgeschichte*, woran es uns noch fast gänzlich fehlt, würde uns die Veränderung der Erdgestalt, imgleichen die der Erdgeschöpfe (Pflanzen und Thiere), die sie durch natürliche Wanderungen (sic! I take it as a misprint for *Wandelungen*) erlitten haben, und ihre daraus entsprungenen Abartungen von dem Urbilde der Stammgattung lehren. Sie würde vermuthlich eine grosse Menge scheinbar verschiedener Arten zu Racen ebenderselben Gattung zurückführen, und das jetzt so weitläuftigte Schulsystem der Naturbeschreibung in ein physisches System für den Verstand verwandeln.

to plant-creation, from thence to the animal, and ultimately to man, we have seen the form of organization advancing, and with it the faculties and instincts of creatures becoming more diversified, until at last they all became united in the human form, in so far as the latter could comprise them. * * * As the body increases by food, so does the mind by ideas; indeed, we notice here the same laws of assimilation, of growth, and of generation. In a word, an inner spiritual man is being formed within us, which has a nature of its own and which employs the body as an instrument merely. * * * Our humanity is merely a preliminary training, the bud of a blossom to come. Step by step does nature cast off the ignoble and the base, while it builds and adds to the spiritual and continues to fashion the pure and refined with increasing niceness; thus are we in a position to hope from the artist-hand of nature that in that other existence our bud of humanity will also appear in its real and true form of divine manhood." * * *

[Herder's idea of evolution would stand on the whole if his conception of "the spiritual" did not imply a preternatural agent.]

"The present state of man is probably the link of junction between two worlds. * * * Yet man is not to investigate himself in this future state; he is to believe himself into it."

Kant makes no objection whatever to the evolutionary ideas of Herder. But Herder was not free from supernaturalism and from fantastic ideas in reference to the future development of man. He had not yet dropped the dualistic conception of the 'duplicity' of man and believed in the immortality of a distinct spiritual individual within his body. Kant's objection, therefore, is twofold; 1) against Herder's supernaturalism which leads him beyond this world; and, 2) against the descent of *all* species from *one and and the same genus*. He says:

"In the gradation between the different species and individuals of a natural kingdom, nature shows us nothing else than the fact that it abandons individuals to total destruction and preserves the species alone. * * * As concerns that *invisible* kingdom of active and independent forces, we fail to see why the author, after having believed he could confidently infer from organized beings, the existence of the rational principle in man did not rather attribute this principle directly to him merely as spiritual nature, instead of lifting it out of chaos through the structural form of organized matter. * * * As to the gradation of organized beings, our author is not to be too severely reproached, if the scheme has not met the requirements of his conception, which extends so far beyond the limits of this world; for its application even to the natural kingdoms here on earth leads to nothing. The slight differences exhibited when species are compared with reference to their common points of resemblance, are, where there is such great multiplicity, a necessary consequence of just this multiplicity. The assumption of common kinship between them, inasmuch as one kind would have to spring from another and all from one original and primitive species, or from one and the same creative source (Mutterschoss)—the assumption of such a common kinship would lead to ideas so strange that reason shrinks from them, and we cannot attribute this idea to the author without doing him injustice. Concerning his suggestions in comparative anatomy through all species down to plants, the workers in natural science must judge for themselves whether the hints given for new observations, will be useful and whether they are justified. * * * It is desirable that our ingenious author who in the continuation of his work will find more *terra firma*, may somewhat restrain his bright genius, and that philosophy (which consists rather in pruning than in fostering luxuriant growth), may lead him to the perfection of his labors not through hints but through definite conceptions, not by imagination but by observation, not by a metaphysical or emotional phantasy but by reason, broad in its plan but careful in its work."

Kant rejected certain conceptions of evolution, but he did not at all show himself averse to the idea in general. He touched upon the subject only incidentally and it is certain that he did not especially favor or entertain the belief in a non-evolutionary origin of living beings.

Before proceeding to the main points of his criticism, Mr. Spencer calls attention to what he designates as Kant's *abnormal* reasoning. Mr. Spencer says:

> "Something must be said concerning abnormal reasoning as "compared with normal reasoning." * * *
>
> "Instead of setting out with a proposition of which the negation is inconceivable, it sets out with a proposition of which the "affirmation is inconceivable, and therefrom proceeds to draw con-"clusions." * * *
>
> "The first sentence in Kant's first chapter runs thus: 'Noth-"ing can possibly be conceived in the world, or even out of it, "which can be called good without qualification, except a Good "Will.'" * * *
>
> "Most fallacies result from the habit of using words without "fully rendering them into thoughts—passing them by with recog-"nitions of their meanings as ordinarily used, without stopping to "consider whether these meanings admit of being given to them in "the cases named. Let us not rest satisfied with thinking vaguely "of what is understood by 'a Good Will,' but let us interpret the "words definitely. Will implies the consciousness of some end to "be achieved. Exclude from it every idea of purpose, and the con-"ception of Will disappears. An end of some kind being necessa-"rily implied by the conception of Will, the quality of the Will is "determined by the quality of the end contemplated. Will itself, "considered apart from any distinguishing epithet, is not cognizable "by Morality at all. It becomes cognizable by Morality only when "it gains its character as good or bad by virtue of its contemplated "end as good or bad." * * *
>
> "Kant tells us that a good will is one that is good in and for "itself without reference to ends."

It is unfortunate that Mr. Spencer misunderstood the first sentence of Kant's book (*Grundlegung zur Metaphysik der Sitten*). Kant does not speak of "a good will without qualification," nor does the expression "without qualification" refer to "a will without reference to ends." Kant speaks of good will in opposition to other good things. Nothing, he says, can without qualification (*ohne Einschränkung*) be called good, except a good will.* Dr. Porter sums up the first page of Kant's essay in the following words:

"The first section of the treatise opens with the memorable and often-quoted utterance, that 'nothing can be possibly conceived in the world, or even out of it, which can be called good without qualification, except a good will.' If character is compared with gifts of nature, as intelligence, courage, and gifts of fortune, as riches, health, or contentment, all these are defective, 'if there is not a good will to correct their possible perversion and to rectify the whole principle of acting, and *adapt it to its end.*' † A man who is endowed with every other good can never give pleasure to an impartial, rational spectator unless he possesses a good will. 'Thus a good will appears to constitute the indispensable condition of being worthy of happiness.' * * * 'Moreover, a good will is good not for what it effects but for what it intends, even when it fails to accomplish its purposes, * * * as when the man wills the good of another and is impotent to promote it, or actually effects just the opposite of what he proposes or wills.'"

In the passages quoted by Dr. Porter, Kant speaks of "the *end* to which good will adapts other goods"; and in another passage of the same book, Kant directly declares that "it is the *end* that serves the will as the objective ground of its self-determination." Mr. Spencer must have overlooked these sentences. Kant says:

"The will is conceived as a power of determining itself to action in accordance with the conception of certain laws. And such a power can only be met with in rational beings. *Now it is the END that serves the will as the objective ground of its self-determination*, and this end, if fixed by reason alone, must hold equally good for all rational creatures."

* * *

Mr. Spencer interrupts his essay on the Ethics of

* The original of the first sentence reads: "Es ist überall nichts in der Welt, ja überhaupt auch ausser derselben zu denken möglich, was ohne Einschränkung für gut könnte gehalten werden, als allein ein guter Wille."

† *Italics are ours.*

Kant by a digression on Kant's conception of time and space. It would lead us too far at present if we would follow Mr. Spencer on this ground also. A comparison of Spencer's remarks on the subject with Kant's "Critique of Pure Reason" will show that Kant's view of space and time is radically different from that view which Mr. Spencer represents as the Kantian conception of time and space.

* * *

Kant rejects the idea that happiness is the end and purpose of life and at the same time he declares that ethics must be based not on the pursuit of happiness but on the categorical imperative or more popularly expressed on our sense of duty.

Mr. Spencer argues:

"One of the propositions contained in Kant's first chapter is "that 'we find that the more a cultivated reason applies itself with "deliberate purpose to the enjoyment of life and happiness, so "much the more does the man fail of true satisfaction.'" * * *

"That which Kant should have said is that the *exclusive* pur-"suit of what are distinguished as pleasures and amusements is dis-"appointing." * * *

"It is not, as Kant says, guidance by 'a cultivated reason,' "which leads to disappointment, but guidance by an uncultivated "reason."

The passage quoted by Mr. Spencer from Kant, reads in its context as follows:

"In the physical constitution of an organized being we take it for granted* that no organ for any purpose will be found in it but

*The phrase "we take it for granted" (in the original "nehmen wir es als Grundsatz an)" reads in the translation quoted by Mr. Spencer: "we take it as a fundamental principle." Mr. Spencer objects to the passage declaring that there *are* many organs (such as rudimentary organs) in the construction of organized beings which serve *no* purpose This however does not stand in contradiction to Kant's assumption that organs of organized beings serve a special purpose. The rudimentary organs have under other conditions served a purpose for which they then were fit and well adapted and are disappearing now because no longer used.

such as is also the fittest and best adapted for that purpose. If in a being possessing reason and will, the preservation, the prosperity, in a word, the happiness of that being, constituted the actual purpose of nature, nature had certainly adopted an extremely unwise expedient to this end, had it made the reason of that being the executive agent of its purposes in this matter. For all actions that it had to perform with this end in view, and the whole rule of its conduct, would have been far more exactly prescribed by *instinct*, and this end would have been far more safely attained by this means than can ever take place through the instrumentality of *reason*." * * *

"As a matter of fact we find that the more a cultivated reason occupies itself with the purpose of enjoying life and happiness, the farther does the person possessing it recede from the state of true contentment; and hence there arises in the case of many, and pre-eminently in the case of those most experienced in the exercise of reason, if they are only frank enough to confess it, a certain degree of misology or hate of reason; for after weighing every advantage that they derive, I will not say from the invention of all arts facilitating ordinary luxury, but even from the sciences, (which after all are in their eyes a luxury of the intellect,) they still discover that virtually they have burdened themselves more with toil and trouble than they have gained in point of happiness, and thus, in the end, they are more apt to envy than contemn the commoner type of men who are more immediately subject to the guidance of natural instinct alone, and who do not suffer their reason to influence in any great degree their acts and omissions."

Kant uses the expression "cultivated reason" not in opposition to "uncultivated reason," but "to instinct" as that inherited faculty which teaches a being to live in accordance with nature and its natural conditions, without the interference of thought and reflection.

That uncultivated reason would lead to disappointment, Kant never would have denied. He would have added: "It does more, it leads to a speedy ruin."

But if reason does not produce happiness, what then is the use of reason? Kant answers, reason produces in man the good will.

It is reason which enables man to form abstractions, to think in generalizations and to conceive the import of universal laws. When his will deliberately and consciously conforms to universal laws, it is good. Kant says:

> "Thus will (viz. the good will) can not be the sole and whole Good, but it must still be the highest Good and the condition necessary to everything else, even to all desire of happiness." * * *

> "To know what I have to do in order that my volition be good, requires on my part no far-reaching sagacity. Unexperienced in respect of the course of nature, unable to be prepared for all the occurrences transpiring therein, I simply ask myself: Can'st thou so will, that the maxim of thy conduct may become a universal law? Where it can not become a universal law, there the maxim of thy conduct is reprehensible, and that, too, not by reason of any disadvantage consequent thereupon to thee or even others, but because it is not fit to enter as a principle into a possible enactment of universal laws."

If a maxim of conduct is fit to enter as a principle into a possible enactment of universal laws, it will be found in harmony with the cosmical laws; if not, it must come in conflict with the order of things in the universe. It then cannot stand, and will, if persistently adhered to, lead (perhaps slowly but inevitably) to certain ruin.

Concerning the proposition that happiness may be regarded as the purpose of life Kant in his review of Herder's "Ideen zur Philosophie der Geschichte der Menschheit" Ed. H. IV, p. 190), speaks of the relativity of happiness and its insufficiency as a final aim of life:

> * * * "First of all the happiness of an animal, then that of a child and of a youth, and lastly that of man! In all epochs of human history, as well as among all classes and conditions of the same epoch, that happiness has obtained which was in exact conformity with the individual's ideas and the degree of his habituation to the conditions amid which he was born and raised. Indeed, it is not even possible to form a comparison of the degree of happiness nor to give precedence to one class of men or to one generation over another. * * * If this shadow-picture of happiness....were the actual aim of Providence, every man would have the measure of his own happiness within him. * * * Does the author (Herder) think perhaps that, if the happy inhabitants of Otaheite had never been visited by more civilized peoples and were ordained to live in peaceful indolence for thousands of years to come—that we could give a satisfactory answer to the question why they should exist at all and whether it would not have been just as well that this island should be occupied by happy sheep and cattle as that it should be inhabited by men who are happy only through pure enjoyment?"

Concerning the mission or purpose of humanity and its ultimate realization, Kant interprets Herder's views as follows:

> "It involves no contradiction to say that no individual member of all the offspring of the human race, but that only the species, fully attains its mission (Bestimmung). The mathematician may explain the matter in his way. The philosopher would say: the mission of the human race as a whole is *unceasing progress*, and the perfection (Vollendung) of this mission is a mere idea (although in every aspect a quite useful one) of the aim towards which, in conformity with the design of providence, we are to direct our endeavors."

We learn from the passages quoted from Kant that his idea of good will is neither mystical and supernatural, nor is it vague. It is a conception as logically and definitely defined as any mathematical definition. Good will in the sense in which Kant defines it, is only possible in a reasonable being by the power of its reason. The good will is the intention of conforming to universal principles and thus of being in harmony with the All. This good will is the cornerstone of Kant's ethics; it appears as the categoric imperative of duty, so to act that the maxim of one's conduct may be fit to become a universal law. It is formulated in another passage: "Act so as if the maxim of thy conduct by thy volition were to become a natural law."

It is easily seen that, in Kant's conception, the *ought* of morals (viz. of the categoric imperative) does not stand in contradiction to the *must* of natural laws. Kant's conception is monistic, not dualistic. Kant says:

> "The moral *ought* is man's *inner*, *necessary* volition as being a member of an intelligible world and is *conceived* by him as an ought only in so far as he considers himself also as a member of the sensory world."*

Our way of explaining it would be: Man *feels* in his activity the categoric imperative as an ought. So the snow crystal, if it were possessed of sensation, would *feel* its formation as an "ought." But both are, and to an outside observer will appear, as a "must."

* * *

In the Spencerian system of ethics, which is utilitarianism, the moral maxim or the idea of duty is not distinguished from the feeling of pleasure or pain that accompanies ethical thoughts and acts, and their consequences. This lack of distinction induces Mr. Spencer to consider man's pursuit of happiness as the basis of ethics. Accordingly the aim of ethics, he

* Das moralische Sollen ist also ein eigenes nothwendiges Wollen als Gliedes einer intelligiblen Welt, und wird nur sofern von ihm als Sollen gedacht, als er sich zugleich wie ein Glied der Sinnenwelt betrachtet. Ed. Hartenstein vol IV. p. 303.

maintains, is not the performance of duty, not the realization of the good; to the utilitarian this is only the means. The end of ethics is the greatest happiness of the greatest number.

It is strange that Mr. Spencer's essay contains a passage which, although intended as a point of objection to Kant, is a corroboration of Kant's ethics, and a refutation of Mr. Spencer's own views. While denying the statement that "a cultivated reason, if applied with deliberate purpose to the enjoyment of life and happiness, will fail to produce true satisfaction," Mr. Spencer says:

> "I assert that it is untrue on the strength of personal experi-
> "ences. In the course of my life there have occurred many in-
> "tervals, averaging a month each, in which the pursuit of happi-
> "ness was the sole object, and in which happiness was success-
> "fully pursued. How successfully may be judged from the fact
> "that I would gladly live over again each of those periods
> "without change, an assertion which I certainly cannot make of
> "any portions of my life spent in the daily discharge of duties."

This statement, if it proves anything, proves that happiness is one thing and duty is another; it proves that Kant's theory of ethics, which is based on the discharge of duty and not on the pursuit of happiness. is correct, and that Mr. Spencer's theory which identifies duty with the pursuit of happiness, is wrong.

However, we must in this place express our opinion that Mr. Spencer's statement *cannot* be quite correct. The discharge of duty, unpleasant though the drudgery part of it may have been, was undoubtedly accompanied and followed by a certain satisfaction, which perhaps was less in quantity, but certainly higher in quality than the pleasure derived from the mere pursuit of happiness. And in the valuation of the intrinsic and of the moral worth of pleasures, the quality alone should be taken into consideration, not the quantity. In this sense only can an ethical hedonism or utilitarianism be acceptable. The man whose pleasures and pains are of a higher kind, of a nobler form, and of a better quality, is morally and generally the more evolved man. And then, the basis of ethics would be, not so much pleasure or happiness as the quality of pleasure or happiness; it would be an aspiration to evolve toward a higher plane of life, to shape our lives in nobler forms, and to enjoy nobler, greater, and more spiritual pleasures, or, as Kant says, "unceasing progress."

Mr. Spencer's assertion, if taken in the sense in which it stands, is a contradiction of his ethical theory. But even if Mr. Spencer had declared that the discharge of duty affords a kind of happiness or satisfaction, as it truly does, there would still remain a deep gap between his and Kant's ethics. Mr. Spencer reduces ethics to mere worldly prudence; he says that we must do the good in order to be happy, and for the sake of its utility, and Kant says we must act so as to be in agreement with universal law. Mr. Spencer says:

> "But now, supposing we accept Kant's statement in full, "what is its implication? That happiness is the thing to be "desired, and, in one way or another, the thing to be "achieved." * * *
>
> "An illustration will best show how the matter stands. To a "tyro in archery the instructor says: 'Sir, you must not point "your arrow directly at the target; if you do, you will inevitably "miss it; you must aim high above the target, and you may then "possibly pierce the bull's-eye.' What now is implied by the "warning and the advice? Clearly that the purpose is to hit the "target. Otherwise there is no sense in the remark that it will "be missed if directly aimed at; and no sense in the remark that "to be hit, something higher must be aimed at. Similarly with "happiness. There is no sense in the remark that happiness will

"not be found if it is directly sought, unless happiness is a thing "to be somehow or other obtained." * * *

"So that in this professed repudiation of happiness as an end, "there lies the inavoidable implication that it *is* the end."

The pursuit of happiness is by no means repudiated by Kant as wrong or immoral; it is only maintained to be insufficient as a foundation of ethics. Kant's remark that happiness will not be found if it is directly sought has no reference to his own ethics. Kant, speaking from the standpoint of one who takes the view of utilitarianism, says that if a cultivated reason applies itself to the sole purpose of enjoying life and happiness, it will meet with a failure.*

Any other explanation of the moral *ought* than that from the Good Will, Kant declares to be *heteronomy*. Will would no longer be itself, and the principle of action would lie in something foreign to the will. Kant says:

"Will in such a case would not be a law to itself; but the object by its relation to the will would impose the law upon the will." * * * This would admit of hypothetical imperatives only: "I ought to do a certain thing, because I want something else." The moral and therefore categorical imperative, on the contrary, says: 'I ought to act so or so, even if I had nothing else in view.' For instance: the hypothetical imperative of heteronomy says: 'I ought not to lie, if I ever wish to preserve my honor.' The categorical imperative says: 'I ought not to lie even if it would not in the least bring me to shame.'"

Mr. Spencer quotes the following passage from Kant:

"I omit here all actions which are already recognized as inconsistent with duty, although they may be useful for this or that purpose, for with these the question whether they are done *from duty* can not arise at all, since they even conflict with it. I also set aside those actions which really conform to duty,

* The passage referred to is quoted in full on page 16.

but to which men have *no* direct *inclination*, performing them because they are impelled thereto by some other inclination. For in this case we can readily distinguish whether the action which agrees with duty is done *from duty*, or from a selfish view. It is much harder to make this distinction when the action accords with duty, and the subject has besides a *direct* inclination to it. For example, it is always a matter of duty that a dealer should not overcharge an inexperienced purchaser, and wherever there is much commerce the prudent tradesman does not overcharge, but keeps a fixed price for every one, so that a child buys of him as well as any other. Men are thus *honestly* served; but this is not enough to make us believe that the tradesman has so acted from duty and from principles of honesty: his own advantage required it; it is out of the question in this case to suppose that he might besides have a direct inclination in favor of the buyers, so that, as it were, from love he should give no advantage to one over another [!]. Accordingly the action was done neither from duty nor from direct inclination, but merely with a selfish view.

"On the other hand, it is a duty to maintain one's life, and, in addition, every one has also à direct inclination to do so. But on this account the often anxious care which most men take for it has no intrinsic worth, and their maxim has no moral import. They preserve their life *as duty requires*, no doubt, but not *because duty requires*. On the other hand, if adversity and hopeless sorrow have completely taken away the relish for life; if the unfortunate one, strong in mind, indignant at his fate rather than desponding or dejected, wishes for death, and yet preserves his life without loving it—not from inclination or fear, but from duty—then his maxim has a moral worth.

"To be beneficent when we can is a duty; and besides this, there are many minds so sympathetically constituted that without any other motive of vanity or self-interest, they find a pleasure in spreading joy around them, and can take delight in the satisfaction of others so far as it is their own work. But I maintain that in such a case an action of this kind, however proper, however amiable it may be, has nevertheless no true moral worth, but is on a level with other inclinations" (pp 17–19)

Kant's metaphysics of ethics is to practical ethics what pure mathematics is to applied mathematics, or what logic is to grammar. Kant's method of reasoning *in abstracto* everywhere shows the mathematical bent of his mind. In a foot-note (Editio Hartenstein, IV), p. 258, he says:

> "As pure mathematics is distinguished from applied mathematics and pure logic from applied logic, so may the pure philosophy (the metaphysics) of ethics be distinguished from the applied philosophy of ethics, that is, as applied to human nature. By this distinction of terms it at once appears that ethical principles are not based upon the peculiarities of human nature but that they must be existent by themselves *a priori*,—whence, for human nature, just as well as for *any* rational nature, practical rules can be derived."

Schleiermacher says:

> "A good is any agreement ("unity") of definite sides [certain aspects] of reason and nature. * * * The end of ethical praxis is the highest good, *i. e.*, the sum of all unions of nature and reason. * * * The moral law may be compared to the algebraic formula which (in analytical geometry) determines the course [path] of a curve; the highest good may be compared to the curve itself, and virtue, or moral power, to an instrument arranged for the purpose of constructing the curve according to the formula." (Quoted from a translation of Ueberweg.)

Kant declares in other passages that in examples taken from practical life, it will be difficult to separate clearly and unmistakably the sense of duty as the real moral motive from other motives, inclinations, habits, etc. But such a distinction must be made, if the moral value of motives is to be considered *in abstracto*. This is necessary for a clear conception of the essential features of morality. Mr. Spencer has on other occasions highly praised the power of generalization, which indeed is fundamentally the same faculty, as thinking *in abstracto;* here, however, he does not follow

Kant's argument, but declares "that the assumed distinction between sense of duty and inclination is untenable." He says:

"The very expression *sense* of duty implies that the mental "state signified is a feeling; and if a feeling it must, like other feel-"ings, be gratified by acts of one kind and offended by acts of an "opposite kind. If we take the name conscience, which is equiva-"lent to sense of duty, we see the same thing. The common ex-"pressions 'a tender conscience,' 'a seared conscience,' indicate the "perception that conscience is a feeling—a feeling which has its "satisfactions and dissatisfactions, and which *inclines* a man to acts "which yield the one and avoid the other—produces an *incli-"nation*," (p. 476).

It is quite true that every state of consciousness is a feeling, but we can and must discriminate between consciousness or feeling and the idea or thought which becomes conscious, in which the feeling appears, and which is, so to speak, the special form of a certain feeling. The consciousness and its special form, the feeling and the mental object of feeling, are in reality one and the same. Yet they are different and must *in abstracto* be well distinguished. Mr. Spencer's method is that of generalization, but generalizing can lead to no satisfactory results, if it is not constantly accompanied by discrimination. We must generalize and discriminate.

If a certain group of states of consciousness takes the form of a logical syllogism, it must not be expected that logic will find its explanation in feeling, although it cannot be denied that all the states of consciousness are feelings. Not the feeling in this case is to be explained, but logic. In our generalizations we must discriminate *in abstracto* between the feeling and the idea which feels. We must positively abstract from feeling and cannot consider whether the feeling of logical arguments is pleasant or unpleasant. Mr. Spencer's method of explaining ethics, if applied to logic, would be as follows: "Man's logical sense is a very complex feeling and has developed from simple percepts such as can be observed in the lowest animals; percepts are a higher evolved form of reactions against irritations such as take place in protoplasm. The old method of explaining logic is that of deduction, modern logic will be inductive. Formerly pure logic was considered as a science *a priori*; but the evolution-philosophy shows that logic is developed by steps, it appears *a priori* to the individual now, but it is in reality a consolidated product of multitudinous experiences received mainly by ancestors and added to by self. Logical sense accordingly finds its explanation in most simple feelings. Our conceptions of logically incorrect feelings will be more and more avoided because they will ultimately be found to be unpleasant; logical correctness is striven for because of the feeling of satisfaction that accompanies the conception of a logically correct conclusion."

Sense is feeling, there can be no doubt. Logical sense and mathematical sense are feelings and if a person thinks a mathematical axiom or a logical syllogism or an ethical maxim, he has a feeling. Logical sense of reason is the product of evolution, and it cannot be denied either that one man has a more logical or mathematical or moral sense than another. But it does not follow that an explanation of mathematics, or logic, or ethics, must be derived from feeling pleasure and pain, or happiness. On the contrary we must abstract from feeling altogether and concern ourselves with the object of feeling only, which is the idea or the special form in which and as which feeling appears. States of consciousness (never mind whether they are painful or pleasurable) must be considered as moral if their mental object, *i. e.*, the idea, the thought, the motive, the form in which feeling becomes manifest, is in harmony with the universal order of things.

* * *

Mr. Spencer declares that the world would be intolerable "if Kant's conception of moral worth were displayed universally in men's acts." And it must be acknowledged that Kant's ethics in their logical and irrefutable rigidity not only impressed the literary world of his time with the grandeur and sublimity of ethics; Kant's ethics also astounded, and overwhelmed his readers with awe. Virtue no longer appeared to be the fervid enthusiasm of sentiments; it congealed into the cold idea of duty which can be fixed in abstract rules and will operate like the correctly calculated gear of a machine. Objections have been raised by some of Kant's own disciples; but it must be known that the Kantian view of ethics does not suppress feelings, emotions and inclinations, it excludes them only from an estimation of the moral worth of actions. Kant gave the *coup de grace* to all sentimentality which had taken the lead in ethical questions too long. Mr. Spencer says:

> "If those acts only have moral worth which are done from "a sense of duty * * * we must say that a man's moral "worth is greater in proportion as the strength of his sense of "duty is such that he does the right thing not only apart from "inclination but against inclination. According to Kant, then, "the most moral man is the man * * * who says of another "that which is true though he would like to injure him by a false-"hood; who lends money to his brother though he would prefer to "see him in distress."

Schiller, although an admirer of Kant, makes in

his Xenions a similar objection to this corollary of the ethics of pure reason. He says:

> "Willingly serve I my friends; but 'tis pity, I do it with pleasure.
> And I am really vexed, that there's no virtue in me!"

And he answers in a second distich:

> "There is no other advice than that you try to despise friends,
> And, with disgust, you will do what such a duty demands."

The difficulty is removed under the following consideration: A man with good inclinations is less exposed to temptation than a man with bad inclinations. If both act morally under conditions otherwise the same, the latter has shown greater strength of moral purpose than the former. The former's character (viz., his inherited inclinations and habits which represent the sum total of the moral energies of his ancestors,) is more moral than that of the latter. But the latter deserves more credit than the former for overcoming the temptation; he has in this special act shown more moral strength of will than his more fortunate and morally higher advanced fellow-man. To those who have accepted the Kantian view, Mr. Spencer's and Schiller's objection can serve as a warning, not to lose sight of emotions altogether. Man is not only a reasonable being, he is at the same time a feeling creature. The instinctive faculties of man, the so-called subconscious states, are the basis of his consciousness. They form the roots of his soul from which spring the clear conceptions of his reason. The more man's habits and inclinations agree with morals, the more strength of purpose is left for further ethical advancement and moral progress.

Similar objections have also been made to Kant's mechanical explanation of the origin of the planetary systems and milky ways. It seemed as if the divinity of nature were replaced by the rigid law of gravity. In his poem "The God's of Greece," Schiller complains:

> " Fühllos selbst für ihres Künstlers Ehre,
> Gleich dem todten Schlag der Pendeluhr,
> Dient sie knechtisch dem Gesetz der Schwere,
> Die entgötterte Natur."

> " Dead even to her Master's praise,
> Like lifeless pendulum's vibration,
> Lo, godless Nature now obeys,
> Slave-like, the law of gravitation." *

Such objections are always raised when a scientific explanation destroys the mystic view that a spirit or at least something unexplainable is the supposed cause of certain phenomena. Our sentiments are so closely connected and intimately interwoven with our errors that truth appears hostile to sentiment, and it becomes difficult to part with errors sanctified by emotion. Sentimentality always complains that clear thought is an enemy of romanticism, and romanticism is the only possible poetry to the taste of the sentimental.

Now it cannot be denied that a one-sided knowledge not only appears rigid, it truly *is* so, and will be destructive of such emotions as reverence, awe, aesthetic taste, religion and art. Criticism is a most essential feature of science and philosophy, and how negative, how desolate and melancholy appear the results of criticism! But the pruning process of criticism is very wholesome, and true science will only profit by discarding the vagueness of indistinct conceptions. Alpine lakes that are really deep can only gain by lucidity. Thus the clearness of genuine science and broad philosophy will only show the depth of truth into which by all its lucidity our emotions can

* Slightly altered from B. W. Ball's translation in The Open Court, p. 83.

plunge without ever finding it shallow or fathoming it in all its profundity.

Agnosticism is like a shallow mud-puddle in which short-sized men can wade without fear of ever going beyond their depth. When the waters are disturbed one cannot see the bottom, and the pool gains the appearance of unfathomable profundity. Mr. Spencer, as we shall see in the third article of this booklet, confounds the basic ideas involved in the problems of philosophy and renders the clearest conceptions inscrutable and mysterious. When all issues are mixed up in inextricable confusion, he exults with joy and concludes that everything is absolutely unknowable.

* * *

Kant's doctrine of ethics is a truth that can stand the severest test.

Ethics, in the sense of the word as used by Kant, can be found in man only, in so far as he is a reasonable being. A truly reasonable being does not allow himself to be guided by impulses but is led by maxims. Inclinations and habits are remnants of instinct. Not he who in instinctive good-naturedness acts morally, is the ethical man, but he who deliberately and consciously considers himself a representative of the general order of things. The man who adopts such maxims as can become universal principles, identifies his will with the laws of the universe. Man's moral dignity must not be sought in vague feelings or in instinctive inspirations; it is based upon his reason and is developed in so far only as he makes use of his reason.

KANT ON EVOLUTION.

IT is very strange that Mr. Herbert Spencer will again and again attack the philosophy and ethics of Kant for views which Kant never held.* It is possible that there are disciples of Kant who deny the theory of evolution. Yet it is certain that Kant himself is not guilty of this mistake. Thinkers who reject the theory of evolution are in this respect as little entitled to call themselves disciples of Kant as, for instance, the Sadducees were to call themselves followers of Christ. Kantian philosophy was foremost in the recognition of the need of evolution, and that at a time when public interest was not as yet centered upon it.

Mr. Spencer's merits in the propagation of the theory of evolution are undeniable, and he deserves our warmest respect and thanks for the indefatigable zeal he has shown in the performance of this great work, for the labors he has undergone, and the sacrifices he has made for it. Yet recognising all that Mr. Spencer has done, we should not be blind to the fact that Kant's conception of evolution is even at the present day more in conformity with the facts of natural science than Mr. Spencer's philosophy, although the latter commonly goes by the name of the philosophy of evolution.

It is painful to note that in many places where Mr. Spencer refers to Kant's philosophy, he does it slightingly, as though Kant were one of the most irrational of thinkers. Kant's reasoning is denounced as "abnormal" and "vicious." I find such phrases as, "It

* See Mr. Spencer's article in *Mind*, No. LIX, p. 313.

is a vice of Kant's philosophy . . . .," "If Kant had known more of Man than he did . . . .," etc. Mr. Spencer characterises Kant's method as follows:

> "Instead of setting out with a proposition of which the negative is inconceivable, it sets out with a proposition of which the affirmation is inconceivable, and proceeds to draw conclusions therefrom."

These attacks of Mr. Spencer on Kant are not justifiable. Kant is not guilty of the faults for which he is arraigned by Mr. Spencer.

* * *

It is, however, fair to state that these misunderstandings appear excusable if the difficulties are borne in mind with which the English student of Kant is confronted. First, Kant cannot be understood without taking into consideration the historical development of his philosophy, and, secondly, most translations of the fundamental terms, he employs, are so misleading that errors can scarcely be avoided.

Kant's philosophy is by no means a perfected system; it rather represents (as perhaps necessarily all philosophies do) the development of a thinker's mind. The "Critique of Pure Reason" especially shows traces of the state of Kant's mind at different periods, and thus it is that we discover passages which closely considered will be found to be contradictory. When reading this remarkable work we feel like travelers walking over the petrified relics of a powerful eruption. There are strata of ideas of the oldest formation close to the thoughts of a recent date. There are also vestiges of intermediate phases. Here they stand in the petrification of printed words, peacefully side by side, as memorials of a great revolution in the development of human thought. It is this state of things which more than anything else makes of Kant's writings such difficult reading. At the same time it is obvious that we cannot simply take the results of Kant's philosophy; we must follow him in the paths by which he arrived at any given proposition.

There is no philosopher that has been worse misinterpreted than Kant; and the English interpreters of Kant have succeeded in mutilating his best thoughts so that this hero of progress appears as a stronghold of antiquated views. Mistranslations or misconceptions of his terms are to a great extent the cause of this singular fate. As an instance we mention the errors that attach to Kant's term *Anschauung*. *Anschauung* is the present object of our senses; it is the impression a man has from looking at a thing and might have been translated by "perception" or perhaps "sensation." It is usually translated by "intuition." The *Anschauung* of objects comprises the data of knowledge, and they are previous to our reflection upon them. An intuition in the sense of the English Intuitionalists is defined as "a presentation which can be given previously to all thought," yet this presentation is supposed to be a kind of revelation, a knowledge that comes to us without our contemplation, a cognition the character of which is immediate as well as mysterious; in short something that is supernatural.

How different is Kant's philosophy, for instance, if his position with reference to time and space is mistaken! "Time and Space are our *Anschauung*," Kant says. But his English translators declare: "Kant maintained that space and time are intuitions." What a difference it makes if intuition is interpreted in the sense applied to it by the English Intuitionalist School instead of its being taken in the original meaning of the word *Anschauung*.

* * *

Any one who knows Kant through Mr. Spencer's representations only, must look upon him as having the most perverse mind that could possibly exist; and yet it is Kant from whom Spencer has indirectly derived the most characteristic feature of his philosophy. What is Mr. Spencer's agnosticism but a popularisation of Kant's view that things in themselves are unknowable?

We conclude from the animosity which Mr. Spencer shows toward Kant that he does not know how much in this respect he agrees with Kant, how much he has unconsciously imbibed from the *Zeitgeist* which in part was formed under the influence of this huge error of the great philosopher.

I feel confident that any clear thinker who studies Kant and arrives along with him at the "thing in itself" will soon free himself from this error of Kantian thought. Kant himself suggests to us the method by which we are to find the way out of agnosticism. As a proof I quote the views of two independent thinkers; both influenced by Kant's criticism but neither a blind follower. Professor Mach says:

> "I have always felt it as a special good fortune, that early in my life, at about the age of fifteen, I happened to find in the library of my father Kant's 'Prolegomena to Any Future Metaphysic.' The book made at that time a powerful, ineffaceable impression upon me that I never afterwards experienced to the same degree in any of my philosophical reading. Some two or three years later I suddenly discovered the superfluous rôle that 'the thing in itself' plays." *The Monist*, Vol. I, No. 1, pp. 65 and 66.

And Schiller guided by similar considerations says in one of his Xenions:

> "Since Metaphysics, of late, without heirs to her fathers was gathered:
> Under the hammer are now 'things in themselves' to be sold."

The latest attack of Mr. Spencer upon Kantism is in the article "Our Space-Consciousness," in *Mind*, written in reply to Professor Watson. Mr. Spencer there repeats his misconception of Kantism, so that I feel urged to utter a few words of protest against his gross misrepresentation of Kant's views. I shall confine myself mainly to quotations from Kant's works—and the passages quoted will speak for themselves. Should there indeed be any disciples of Kant who are, as Mr. Spencer says, "profoundly averse to that evolutionary view which contemplates mind as having had a genesis conforming to laws like those conformed to by the genesis of the body," these quotations will suffice to prove that they have misconstrued the views of their master. Philosophers hostile to the theory of evolution had better select another patron for their ideas. Kant is too radical a mind to protect those men who in the domains of thought give the signal for retreat.

Mr. Spencer adopted the evolution theory as it was presented by Von Baer, who explains "*Entwickelung*" as a progress from the homogeneous to the heterogeneous.

Baer's "Developmental History of Animals" was published in 1828. Mr. Spencer adopted the theory in 1854. But the history of the theory of evolution is older than Von Baer's book. Professor Baer concludes his work with a few corollaries among which near the end we find the following passage:

"If we survey the contents of the whole Scholia, there follows from them a general result. We found that the effect of generation continues to advance from a part to a whole [Schol. 2.]; that in development, self-dependence increases in correspondence with its environment [Schol. 2.], as well as the determinateness of its structure [Schol. 1.]; that in the internal development special parts shape themselves forth from the more general, and their differentiation increases [Schol. 3.]; that the individual, as the possessor of a fixed organic form, changes by degrees from more general forms into more special [Schol. 5.].

"The general result of our inquiry and consideration can now well be declared as follows:

> "That the developmental history of the individual is the history of increasing individuality in every relation; that is, Individualisation.

"This general conclusion is, indeed, so plain, that it needs no proof from observation, but seems evident *a priori*. But we believe that this evidentness is merely the stamp of truth, and therefore is its guarantee. Had the history of development from the outset been perceived as just expressed, it could and should have been inferred, that the individual of a determinate animal type attains to this by changing from a general into a special form. But experience teaches everywhere, that deductions are always safer if their results are discovered beforehand hy observation. Mankind would have obtained a still greater intellectual possession than it really has, had this been otherwise.

"But if this general conclusion has truth and contents, it is *one fundamental idea* which runs through all forms and degrees of animal development, and governs every single relation. It is the same idea that collected in space the distributed particles into spheres and united them in solar systems; which caused the disintegrated dust on the surface of our metallic planet to grow up into living forms; but this idea is nothing else than life itself, and the words and syllables in which it expresses itself, are the different forms of life."

These corollaries were not inserted by Baer because he intended to proclaim a new truth, but simply to excite a popular interest in a strictly scientific work, in order to extend the circle of its readers. Baer says in the preface:

"So much about the first part. In order to procure for the work readers and buyers, I have added a second part in which I make some general remarks under the title of Scholia and Corollaries. They are intended to be sketches of the confession of my scientific faith concerning the development of animals, as it was formed from the observation of the chick and by other inquiries.',

The *Encyclopædia Britannica* says of Baer, "he prepared the way for Mr. *Spencer's generalisation* of the law of organic evolution as the law of all evolution.*

Baer declares that individualisation is "the one fundamental idea that goes through *all* the forms of cosmic and animal development." The generality of the law of evolution is clearer in the language employed by Baer, in the full context of the Scholia than appears from the short statement of the *Encyclopædia Britannica.* Nevertheless, it is clear enough in the quoted passage that Baer made a statement of universal application. How can such a universal statement be made more general?

Some zealous Spencerians claim that Mr. Spencer is the discoverer of the theory of evolution, but their pretension is only an evidence of grossest ignorance. Mr. Spencer had some second-hand information of Von Baer's *Entwickelungsgeschichte* and his adoption of Von Baer's view, that development is a progress from the homogeneous to the heterogeneous, (which is only partly true,)† cannot be called a discovery. The history of the discovery of the theory of evolution begins about a century before Mr. Spencer appropriated the idea and announced himself as its champion.

*The whole passage reads: "In his *Entwickelungsgeschichte der Thiere*, p. 264, he distinctly tells us that the law of growing individuality is the 'fundamental thought which goes through all forms and degrees of animal development and all single relations. It is the same thought which collected in the cosmic space solar systems; the same which caused the weather-beaten dust on the surface of our metallic planet to spring forth living beings.' Von Baer thus prepared the way for Mr. Spencer's generalisation of the law of organic evolution as the law of all evolution." (*Enc. Brit.*, Vol. VIII., p. 763.)

†Cf. "The Test of Progress" in *Homilies of Science*, pp. 36-42.

In Kant's time the interest in the theory of evolution was confined to a few minds. It is well known that Goethe was one of its most enthusiastic supporters.* In the middle of the eighteenth century there were three views proposed to explain the origin and the development of organised beings: (1) Occasionalism, (2) the theory of Evolution, and (3) the theory of Epigenesis. Occasionalism maintained that God created on each new occasion a new animal. The word evolution was used in a different sense from that in which it is now understood: evolutionism, as maintained by Bonnet, Haller, and others, was the view that the sperma contained a very small specimen of the animal that was to grow from it. The hen's egg was supposed to contain an excessively minute but complete chicken. The theory of epigenesis, however, propounded in 1759 by Caspar Friedrich Wolff in his "Theoria Generationis," explained development by additional growth, and it is this theory of epigenesis which later on, after the total defeat of the old evolutionism, was called (but improperly) the evolution theory. The word "evolution" has thus again admitted the erroneous idea of an unfolding.

In Kant's time the battle between the occasionalists, the evolutionists, and the adherents of the epigenesis theory was hot indeed; and Kant unquestionably gave preference to the epigenesis theory. The most important passage on the subject appears in his "Critique of Judgment." It is as follows:

"If now the teleological principle of the generation of organised beings be accepted, as it would be, we can account for their internally adapted form either by *Occasionalism* or by *Prestabilism.*†

* See Haeckel, *Goethe on Evolution*, No. 131 of *The Open Court*.

† *Præstabilismus*, that is, the theory that the phenomena of nature are the result of pre-established law.

According to the first, the supreme world-cause would, in agreement with its idea, on the occasion of every coition directly give the proper organic form to the material thereby blended; according to the second, it would have implanted into the original products of its designing wisdom merely the power by means of which an organic being produces its like and the species itself is constantly maintained and likewise the death of individuals is continually replaced by their own nature, which is operating at the same time for their destruction.

"If we assume occasionalism for the production of organised beings, nature is thereby wholly discarded, and with it the use of reasoning in determining the possibility of such kinds of products; therefore, it cannot be supposed that this system is accepted by any one who has had to do with philosophy."

"As to *Prestabilism*, it can proceed in a two-fold manner, namely, it considers every organic being produced by its like, either as the *educt* or as the *product* of the first. The system which considers generated beings as mere *educts* is called that of *individual preformation*, or also the *theory of evolution;* that which makes generated beings *products* is named the system of *epigenesis*. The latter can also be called a system of *generic preformation*, because the productive power of those generating was virtually preformed to agree with the internal adapted arrangements that fell to the lot of their race. The opposing theory to this view should be named that of individual preformation, or still better, the *theory of evolution*."

"The defenders of the theory of evolution, who exempt each individual from the formative power of nature, in order to derive the same directly from the hand of the Creator, would not dare to permit this to happen in accordance with the hypothesis of occasionalism, so that coition would be a mere formality, a supreme national world-cause having decided to form every particular fœtus by direct interference, and to resign to the mother only its development and nourishment. They declared themselves in favor of preformation, *as though it were not the same to make the required forms arise in a supernatural manner at the beginning of the world, as during its progress;* and as if a great multitude of supernatural arrangements would not rather be dispensed with through occasional creation which were necessary in order that the embryo formed at the beginning of the world should, throughout the long period up to its development, not suffer from the destructive forces of nature, but endure and maintain itself intact; moreover, an immensely greater number of such preformed beings would be made than ever would be developed, and with them as many creations be thus rendered unnecessary and purposeless. They still, however, resign at least something to nature, in order not to fall in with complete hyperphysics, which can dispense with explanation from nature. They still held fast indeed, to their hyperphysics; even finding in monsters (which it must be impossible to regard as designs of nature) cases of adaptation which call for admiration, although the only purpose of that adaptedness might be to make an anatomist take offence at it as a purposeless adaptedness, and have a sense of melancholy admiration. Yet they could not well fit the generation of hybrids into the system of preformation, but were obliged still further to endow the sperm of male creatures with a designedly acting power, whereas they had otherwise accorded it nothing except mechanical force to serve as the first means of nourishment of the embryo; yet this designedly acting force, in the case of the products of generation between two creatures of the same kind, they would grant to neither of them.

"If on the contrary the great advantage was not at once recognised which the theory of epigenesis possessed over the former in view of the experimental foundation on which the proof of it rested; yet reason would be especially favorably predisposed from the outset for this mode of explanation, inasmuch as it regards nature—with reference to the things which originally can be conceived as possible only in accordance with the theory of causality and design, at least so far as propagation is concerned—as self-producing and not merely as developing, and thus with the least possible employment of the supernatural, leaves all that comes afterwards, from the very beginning on, to nature: without concerning itself with the original beginning, with regard to the explanation of which physics in general miscarries, try with what chain of causes it may."

Kant recognises neither the stability of species nor any fixed limits between them. And this one maxim alone suffices to prove that he was of the same opinion as the great biologist who wrote the "Origin of Species." Kant says (Ed. Hart. III. p. 444):

"*Non datur vacuum formarum*, that is, there are not different original and primitive species, which were, so to say, isolated and separated by an empty space from one another, but all the manifold species are only divisions of a single, chief, and general species; and from this principle results again this immediate inference: *datur continuum formarum*, that is, all differences of species border on each other, and allow no transition to one another by a leap, but only through very small degrees of difference, by which we can arrive at one from another; in one word, there are no species or sub-species which, according to reason, would be *next* each other in affinity, but intermediate species are always possible, whose difference from the first and second is less than their difference from one another."

In Kant's "Critique of Judgment" (§. 80) we find the following passage:

"The agreement of so many species of animals, with reference to a definite, common scheme, which appears not only to be at the foundation of their bony structure, but also of the arrangement of their other parts, in which, by abridgment of one and prolongation of another, by envelopment of this and unfolding of that, a wonderful simplicity of plan has been able to produce so great a diversity of species—this agreement casts a ray of hope, although a weak one, in the mind, that here, indeed, something might be accomplished with the principle of the mechanism of nature, without which in general there can be no physical science.

"This analogy of forms, so far as they appear, notwithstanding all their diversity, to be produced after the model of a common prototype, strengthens the conjecture of a real relationship between the same by generation from a common ancestral source, through the gradual approach of one animal species to another, from man, in whom the principle of design appears to be best proved, to the polyp, from this to the moss and lichen, and finally to the lowest stage of nature perceptible to us, to crude matter, from which and its forces, according to mechanical laws (like those which work in the production of crystals), the whole technic of nature (which is so incomprehensible to us in organised beings that we imagine another principle is necessitated for their explanation) appears to be derived.

"The Archæologist of nature is now free to make that great family of beings (for such we must conceive it, if the uninterrupted relationship is to have a foundation) arise out of the extant vestiges of the oldest revolutions, following every mechanism known to him or which he can suppose."

Kant adds in a footnote:

"An hypothesis of such a kind can be named a daring venture of reason, and there may be few of the most sagacious naturalists, through whose minds it has not sometimes passed. For it is not absurd, as the *generatio equivoca*, by which is understood the production of an organised being through the mechanical action of crude unorganised matter. But it would still be *generatio univoca* in the common understanding of the word, in so far only as something organic was produced out of another organic body, although specifically distinguished from it; for instance, if certain aquatic animals by and by formed into amphibia, and from these after some generations into land animals. *A priori* this does not contradict the judgment of pure reason. Only experience shows no example thereof; according to it, rather, all generation which we know is *generatio homonyma* (not mere *univoca* in opposition to production out of unorganised material), that is, the bringing forth of a product homogeneous in organisation, with the generator: and *generatio heteronyma*, so far as our actual experience of nature goes is nowhere met with."

The treatise "Presumable Origin of Humanity," Kant sums up in the following sentence:

"From this representation of the earliest human history it results that man's departure from the first abode of his kind represented in his judgment as Paradise, was no other than the transition of mere animal creatures out of barbarism into man, out of the leading-strings of instinct into the guidance of reason, in a word, out of the guardianship of nature into the state of freedom."

In his work "Upon the Different Races of Mankind," Kant discusses the origin of the species of man in a way which would do honor to a follower of Darwin. It is written in a spirit which recognises the difference of conditions as the causes that produce different species, and the very distinction which he makes between "natural science" as purely descriptive, and "natural history" as treating "the natural transformations and arising therefrom the departures from the prototype,"* is the best evidence that Kant supported the principle of the theory of evolution. Natural history, according to Kant's definition, is an exposition of the evolution of species, and he rightly claims that in his time it was "almost entirely lacking." A beginning was made by himself when he wrote his *General History and Theory of the Heavens.* This book alone, in which he propounded a theory of the evolution of the stellar universe "according to mechanical law," entitles Kant to be called an evolutionist.†

Kant claims that natural history (or, as we should say now, the doctrine of evolution) "would probably trace a great number of apparently different varieties back to a species of one and the same kind."

Kant had quite a definite idea, not only of the evolution of man, but also of the survival of the fittest. He says:

* The passage is quoted in full on page 9.

† Kant's *Allgemeine Naturgeschichte und Theorie des Himmels* appeared anonymously in 1755. We speak of the Kant-Laplace theory, but, says John B. Stallo in his excellent book, *Concepts of Modern Physics*, p. 280: "The truth is that the nebular hypothesis in the form in which it is now generally held is due to Kant, and differs in several essential particulars from the hypothesis of Laplace." Laplace published his work, *Exposition du système du monde* (styled by Arago *Mécanique céleste*) in 1796, and, strange to say, the French astronomer knew nothing of the propositions of his anticipator. Laplace declares that "the atmosphere of the sun at one time extended beyond the orbits of the farthest planets, and that their formation is due to a gradua cooling and contracting of this solar system." Laplace's idea is fully and almost literally contained in Kant's work, which is broader and states the universal law of world-formation.

"The cry which a child scarcely born utters, has not the tone of misery, but of irritation, and violent rage; not the result of pain, but of vexation about something; probably for the reason that it wishes to move itself and feels its incapacity, like a captive when freedom is taken from him. What purpose can nature have in providing that a child shall come with a loud cry into the world, which for it and the mother is, in the *rude natural state*, full of danger? Since a wolf, a pig even, would in the absence of the mother, or through her feebleness owing to her delivery, be thus attracted to devour it. But no animal except man as he now is announces with noise its new-born existence; which in the wisdom of nature appears to be arranged *in order that the species shall be preserved*. We must also assume that in what was an early epoch of nature for this class of animals (namely in the period of barbarism) this outcry of the child at its birth did not exist; consequently only later on a second epoch appeared, after both parents had arrived at that degree of civilisation which was required for home-life; yet without knowing how and by what interweaving causes nature arranges such a development. This remark leads us far; for example, to the thought whether after the same epoch, still a third did not follow accompanied by great natural revolutions, during which an orang-outang or a chimpanzee perfected the organs which serve for walking, for feeling objects, and for speech, and thus evolved the limb-structure of man; in which animals was contained an organ for the exercise of the function of reason, which by social cultivation was gradually perfected and developed."

Kant's view concerning the origin of the biped man from quadruped animal ancestors is most unequivocally stated.

In a review of Dr. Moscati's Lecture upon the difference of structure in animals and in men, Kant says:

"Dr. Moscati proves that the upright walk of man is constrained and unnatural; that he is indeed so constructed that he may be able to maintain and move in this position, but that, although by needful and constant habit he formed himself thus, inconvenience and disease arise therefrom, which sufficiently prove, that he was misled by reason and imitation to deviate from the first animal arrangement. Man is not constructed internally different from other animals that go on all fours. When now he raises himself his intestines, particularly the embryo of pregnant individuals, come into a pendulous situation and a half reversed condition, which, if it often alternates with the lying position or that on all-fours, cannot precisely produce specially evil consequences, but, by constant continuance, causes deformities and numerous diseases. Thus, for example, the heart, because it is compelled to hang free, elongates the blood vessels to which it is attached, assumes an oblique position since it is supported by the diaphragm and slides with its end against the left side—a position wherein man, especially at full growth, differs from all other animals, and thereby receives an inevitable inclination to aneurism, palpitation, asthma, chest-dropsy, etc., etc. With the upright position of man the mesentery, pulled down by the weight of the intestines, sinks perpendicularly thereunder, is elongated and weakened, and prepared for numerous ruptures. In the mesenteric vein which has no valves, the blood moves slowly and with greater difficulty (it having to ascend against the course of gravity) than would happen with the horizontal position of the trunk. . . ."

"We could add considerably to the reasons just adduced to show that our animal nature is really quadrupedal. Among all four-footed animals there is not a single one that could not swim if it accidentally fell into the water. Man alone drowns, except in cases where he has learned to swim. The reason is because he has laid aside the habit of going on all-fours; for it is by this motion that he would keep himself up in the water without the exercise of any art, and by which all four-footed creatures, who otherwise shun the water, swim. . . ."

"It will be seen, accordingly, that the first care of nature was that man should be preserved as animal for *himself and his species*, and for that end the position best adapted to his internal structure, to the lay of the fœtus, and to his preservation in danger, was the quadrupedal position; we see, moreover, that a germ of reason is placed in him, whereby, after the development of the same, he is destined for *social intercourse*, and by the aid of which he assumes the position which is in every case the most fitted for this, namely, the bipedal position,—thus gaining upon the one hand infinite advantages over animals, but also being obliged to put up with many inconveniences that result from his holding his head so proudly above his old companions."

In the double-leaded quotation on pages 43 and 44 Kant speaks about the explanation of organised life from man down to the polyp "according to mechanical laws like those which work in the production of crystals," and he adds, in organised beings the whole technic of nature is so incomprehensible to us "that we imagine another principle is necessitated for their explanation."

This "other principle" would be the principle of design, or the teleological explanation of phenomena. In his old age Kant inclined more to teleology than in his younger years, and it is for this reason that Professor Ernst Haeckel accuses Kant of inconsistency.

After having pointed out that "Kant is one of the few philosophers that combine a well-founded knowledge of the natural sciences with extraordinary precicision and depth of speculation" and further that "he was the first who taught 'the principle of the struggle for existence' and 'the theory of selection.'" Haeckel says in his "Natürliche Schöpfungsgeschichte," 8th edition, p. 91:

"Wir würden daher unbedingt in der Geschichte der Entwickelungslehre unserem gewaltigen Königsberger Philosophen den ersten Platz einräumen müssen, wenn nicht leider diese bewundernswürdigen monistischen Ideen des jungen Kant später durch den überwältigenden Einfluss der dualistisch christlichen Weltanschauung ganz zurückgedrängt worden wären."

This "influence of the dualistic Christian world-conception" is according to Haeckel, Kant's recognition of a teleological causation in the realm of organised life. Haeckel says in the same place:

"Er behauptet, dass sich im Gebiete der anorganischen Natur unbedingt sämmtliche Erscheinungen aus mechanischen Ursachen, aus bewegenden Kräften der Materie selbst, erklären lassen, im Gebiete der anorganischen Natur dagegen nicht."

Haeckel does not stand alone in denouncing the old Kant. Schopenhauer distinguishes between the author of the first and the author of the second edition of the "Critique of Pure Reason," regarding the former only as the real Kant. These accusations are not without foundation, but we believe with Max Müller that they have been unduly exaggerated.

As to teleology for which Kant's preference appears to be more strongly marked in his later than in his younger years we should say that it is a problem that should, in an historical investigation, as to whether or not Kant was a consistent evolutionist, be treated independently. No one can deny that there is an adaptation to ends in the domain of organised life. It is not so much required to deny teleology in the domain of organised nature as to purify and critically sift our views of teleology. There is a kind of teleology which does not stand in contradiction to the causation of efficient causes so called.

Mr. Spencer's denunciations of Kant would have some foundation, if he had reference to the old Kant alone. But everyone who censures Kant for the errors of his later period is bound to qualify his statement, and indeed whenever such strictures of Kantism appear I find them expressly stated as having reference to "the old Kant."

That Kant who is a living power even to-day is the young Kant, it is the author of the first edition of the "Critique of Pure Reason." He is generally called "the young Kant," although he was not young; he was, as we say, in his best years. The old Kant who proclaimed that he "must abolish knowledge in order to make room for faith" is a dead weight in our colleges and universities. The young Kant is positive, the old Kant is agnostic. The young Kant was an investigator and naturalist of the first degree; he gave an impetus to investigation that it had never before received from philosophy. The old Kant, I should not exactly say reverted but certainly, neglected the principles of his younger years and thus became the leader of a reactionary movement from which sprang two offshoots very unlike each other but children of the same father; the Oxford transcendentalism as represented by Green and the English agnosticism as represented by Mr. Spencer.

It is strange that Mr. Spencer has so little knowledge concerning the evolution of the views he holds. If he were more familiar with the history of the idea "that the world-problem is insolvable, he would show more reverence toward the old Kant and his mystical inclinations; for Kant, whatever Mr. Spencer may say against it, is the father of modern agnosticism.*]

*
* *

The history of Mr. Spencer's philosophical development shows that the first idea which took possession of his mind and formed the centre of crystalisation for all his later views was M. Condorcet's optimism. Condorcet believed in progress; he was convinced that in spite of all the tribulations and anxie-

* In this connection we call attention to a book, *Kant und Darwin, ein Beitrag zur Geschichte der Entwickelungslehre*, Jena, 1875, by Fritz Schultze, formerly Privat docent in Jena, now Professor of philosophy at the Polytechnic Institute in Dresden. This little book is a collection of the most important passages of Kant's views concerning evolution, the struggle for existence, and the theory of selection, and it is astonishing to find how much Kant had to say on the subject and how strongly he agrees with and anticipates Darwin. If Kant had not lived before Darwin one might be tempted to conclude that he was familiar with his *Origin of Species* and *The Descent of Man.*

ties of the present, man would at last arrive at a state of perfection. He saw a millennium in his prophetic mind, which alas!—if the law of evolution be true—can never be realised. Condorcet died a martyr to his ideals. He poisoned himself in 1799 to escape death by the Guillotine.

The influence of Condorcet's work *Esquisse d'un tableau historique des progrès de l'esprit humain* is traceable not only in Mr. Spencer's first book, "Social Statics," published in 1850, but in all his later writings. How can a true evolutionist believe in the Utopia of a state of perfect adaptation? Does not each progress demand new adaptations? Take as an instance the change from walking on four feet to an upright gait. Did not this progress itself involve man in new difficulties, to which he had to adapt himself? Let a labor-saving machine be invented, how many laborers lose their work and how many others are in demand! The transition from one state to the other is not easy, and as soon as it is perfected new wants have arisen which inexorably drive humanity onward on the infinite path of progress which can never be limited by any state of perfection. There is a constant readjustment necessary, and if we really could reach a state of perfect adaptation human life would drop into the unconsciousness of mere reflex motions.

Any one who understands the principle of evolution and its universal applicability, will recognise that there can be no standstill in the world, no state of perfect adaptation. Our solar system has evolved, as Kant explained in his "General Cosmogony and Theory of the Heavens," out of a nebula, and is going to dissolve again into a nebular state. So our social development consists in a constant realisation of ideals.

We may think that if we but attain our next and dearest ideal, humanity will be satisfied forever. But as soon as we have realised that ideal, we quickly get accustomed to its benefits. It becomes a matter of course and another ideal higher still than that just realised appears before our mental gaze.

Herder, in his "Ideas for a Philosophy of the History of Mankind," not unlike Mr. Spencer, was also under the spell of the Utopian ideal, that humanity will reach at last a state of perfect happiness. Kant, in his review of Herder's book, discusses the relativity of happiness and its insufficiency as a final aim of life. He says:

"First of all the happiness of an animal, then that of a child and of a youth, and lastly that of man! In all epochs of human history, as well as among all classes and conditions of the same epoch, that happiness has obtained which was in exact conformity with the individual's ideas and the degree of his habituation to the conditions amid which he was born and raised. Indeed, it is not even possible to form a comparison of the degree of happiness nor to give precedence to one class of men or to one generation over another. . . . If this shadow-picture of happiness . . . . were the actual aim of Providence, every man would have the measure of his own happiness within him. . . . Does the author (Herder) think perhaps that, if the happy inhabitants of Otaheiti had never been visited by more civilised peoples and were ordained to live in peaceful indolence for thousands of years to come—that we could give a satisfactory answer to the question why they should exist at all, and whether it would not have been just as well that this island should be occupied by happy sheep and cattle as that it should be inhabited by men who are happy only through pure enjoyment?"

"It involves no contradiction to say that no individual member of all the offspring of the human race, but that only the species, fully attains its mission (Bestimmung). The mathematician may explain the matter in his way. The philosopher would say: the mission of the human race as a whole is *unceasing progress*, and the perfection (Vollendung) of this mission is a mere idea (although in every aspect a very useful one) of the aim towards which in conformity with the design of providence, we are to direct our endeavors."

It is indubitable that Kant's views of evolution agree better with the present state of scientific investigation than does Mr. Spencer's philosophy, which has never been freed from Condorcet's ingenuous optimism. The assumption of a final state of perfection by absolute adaptation is irreconcilable with the idea of unceasing progress, which must be true if evolution is a universal law of nature.

* * *

Soon after the publication of this article, the author's proposition that Kant's writings are difficult reading (made on page 33, line 4) found an unexpected and vigorous opposition.

Mr. Charles S. Peirce made the following incidental remark in a letter to the author (Sept. 6, 1890):

"I have heard too much of Kant's being hard reading. I think he is one of the easiest of philosophers; for he generally knows what he wants to say, which is more than half the battle, and he says it in terms which are very clear. Of course, it is quite absurd to try to read Kant without preliminary studies of Leibnitz and English philosophers, as well as of the terminology of which Kant's is a modification or transmogrification. But there is a way of making out what he meant, while such writers as Hume and J. S. Mill, the more you study them the more they puzzle you."

I agree with Mr. Peirce's proposition, though I should prefer to express it differently. I say Kant is hard reading, but if we read him with care we can easily know what he means. Mr. Spencer's writings are easy reading, but considering the looseness of his thoughts he is difficult to comprehend, and his many contradictory statements are hard to reconcile.

MR. SPENCER'S AGNOSTICISM.

MR. Herbert Spencer as a philosopher and as a thinker is a power in our age, not only because he understands how to deal with deep problems so as to impress his conception of them upon the reader, but also because his views strongly coincide with the *Zeitgeist* of the present generation. I am fully aware of the fact that in some most vital principles the philosophy which I uphold is in perfect sympathy with the spirit of Mr. Spencer's views, but at the same time I recognise that there are points not less important in which there is no agreement, and perhaps the most important one is the doctrine of agnosticism.

Now there is a certain truth in agnosticism, which has been felt and recognised at all times and may be considered as a truism. It is this, that existence exists, and we do not know whence it comes. We may imagine that existence did not exist, and it seems that non-existence ought to be the natural and aboriginal condition. But we do exist; we are here and are a part of a great whole. We can understand how we originated from prior conditions, and can trace the forms of being back indefinitely, but we are utterly incapable of tracing them back to nothingness, and all attempts at deriving existence from non-existence finally end in lamentable failures. Thus the suspicion rises that the question, "Whence does existence come?" itself may be illegitimate.

Prof. W. K. Clifford in his lecture on "Theories of Physical Forces" endeavors to explain the redundancy of the question "Why?" in science. Science teaches that it is so and that it must be so. Given one moment of the world-process, and we can calculate the next following or any other one with certainty: we can say that it must be such or such a state of things. But the "Why?" of things, Clifford says, does not lie in the range of science, for the question has no sense.

Clifford's proposition is directed against metaphysical philosophers to whom there is a "Why?" of facts, that is to say, a reason for the world at large, or as it is sometimes expressed, "a First Cause." Clifford's conception of the "Why?" and the "That," it appears to us, is simply a denunciation of the so called great world-enigma as a sham problem which has no sense.

Goethe makes a similar remark. He says:

> "Wie, Wann, und Wo?—Die Götter bleiben stumm.
> Du halte dich an's Weil und frage nicht Warum."

That is to say, why, when, and where existence originated, are questions which do not admit of any answer. Trace the Because, and leave the Why alone.

We should prefer to say, the tracing of the "that" is the only legitimate conception of the "why?"

The "that," however, appears as a triple enigma, which can be formulated as the problem of creation, of eternity, and infinity. There is the "that" of actuality, the "that" of its extent, and the "that" of its duration.*

Experience teaches us that there is something stir-

*A discussion of Emil Du Bois-Raymond's "Seven World-Riddles' would here lead us too far. That he selected the sacred number "seven" was a pure self-mystification and shows his inclination to mysticism.

ring about. It is as Goethe calls it in the words of Mephistopheles:

> "Was sich dem Nichts entgegenstellt,
> Das Etwas, diese plumpe Welt."

This something stirring about (reduced to general ideas) is substance moving in space, and thus the metaphysical question shows three aspects, the problem of substance, the problem of motion (viz., of causation or succession of events in time), and the problem of space. The question whence they come, where and when they originated, receives no other answer than that they exist; they exist now, have always existed, and will always exist, which finds expression in three negations, three *nots:* substance does *not* rise from nothing, time has *not* either a beginning or an end, space is *not* limited. In other words: substance is uncreate, time is eternal, space is infinite.

Man's reluctance to be satisfied with the fact of the "that," and his expectation to derive facts somehow from nothingness, finds expression in three unwarranted assumptions:

1. The assumption of creation, based on the argument that reality took its rise from non-existence, or else being uncreated should not exist;

2. The assumption of a beginning of the world-process, which must have been caused by some external agent or else could not have started; and

3. The assumption of the limitations of space, an idea expressed in many ancient illustrations of the universe, but now utterly abandoned. Space is supposed to come somewhere to an end, as if it were a big box, and the world is supposed to be contained in it.

It goes without saying that science does not countenance these assumptions. If the "that" of existence is accepted as a given fact, the world-problems lose their metaphysical significance, for the stubbornness of reality is as little mysterious as are the ideas of infinity and eternality.*

To a positivist the three problems are disposed of by the simple recognition of the "that." Positivism starts from facts as the data of cognition, and does not deem itself responsible to explain the "why" of the "that," but traces the "why" *in* the "that." When we know more about the whole of the stellar universe we may be able to say more about its limits in time and space and perhaps also about the irritation that caused the whirls in the primordial ether; but the basic question, why existence exists, whence the ether comes, would remain as it is now. The existence of existence is simply the brutal self-assertion of facts—*das Etwas, diese plumpe Welt!*

Knowledge means a representation of facts in mental symbols, and comprehension means a unification or harmonious systematisation of these symbols. At any rate, we have to start with facts. As soon, however, as we attempt to start with nothing and hope by some sleight of hand to create facts or to evolve them out of non-existence, we are confronted with an insolvable world-problem. Yet the proposition of this world-problem can bear no close investigation. It rests upon a misstatement of the case, for the very demand to produce positive facts out of nothing, is itself contradictory and is as absurd as the idea of a First or Ultimate Cause.

*The idea of infinity has caused a great deal of trouble, but the infinite (if understood in its proper sense, which is that of mathematics) is actually a much simpler conception than the finite. See the author's *Homilies of Science*, pp. 108–111.

The idea of a first cause rests upon a confusion of the terms "cause" and "*raison d'être.*" A first cause cannot exist, because every cause is the effect of a former cause, but we may conceive of an ultimate *raison d'être.* Every *raison d'être* of a natural process is formulated in a natural law, and all these natural laws, if they were all known and investigated, would form one great system of laws which can serve as a means of orientation in this world. The most general of these laws, being the most comprehensive statement of facts, would be the ultimate *raison d'être* or ground of the world.

The idea of an ultimate ground or *raison d'être* of the world is legitimate, but the idea of a "First Cause" is spurious. A First Cause is inscrutable, indeed, not because it is so profound an idea that "it passes all comprehension," but simply because it is a self-contradictory and nonsensical idea.*

* * *

A philosophy which grants that the world exists and builds its world-conception out of the facts of experience, leaving the problem how existence can be derived from non-existence to metaphysicians of the old school, is called Positivism, and a genuine positivism has no need of blocking the way of science with the bugbears of unknowables. But Mr. Spencer makes of the unknowable the cornerstone of his philosophy and is not satisfied until he finds everything incomprehensible, mysterious, and inscrutable. Through the spectacles of his philosophy even science herself proves ultimately a mere systematisation of nescience.

*For further details on the problem of causation see the author's *Fundamental Problems*, pp. 79–91 ff., and *Primer of Philosophy*, pp. 137 ff.

And how does Mr. Spencer succeed in proving his case?

Very simply, by confounding the issues and then drawing the conclusion that the thing under consideration is inscrutable and the problem insolvable.

Mr. Spencer's agnosticism is not a philosophical formulation of the difficulty which presents itself in the stubborn actuality of facts and in our inability to derive existence from non-existence. A general sentiment of this difficulty may have been hidden in the subconscious depths of his soul and have prompted him to embrace and glorify agnosticism, but the agnosticism which he actually proposes, genuine Spencerian agnosticism, consists in a mystery-isation of scientific knowledge itself, brought about by a perversion of scientific methods and an ill-concealed love of the chiaroscuro of a dilettantic sciolism.

In his *First Principles* Mr. Spencer proposes untenable and self-contradictory conceptions of the terms space, time, matter, and motion, and then concludes that they pass all understanding. Mr. Spencer, however, overlooks that all our conceptions are mere abstractions describing certain qualities, that these terms represent these qualities, and comprehension is nothing more or less than a proper and systematic representation. We know what matter, motion, space and time are, if considered as abstractions, although it is true we cannot know what they are in themselves. But we need not know it, for space, time, matter, and motion do not exist in themselves; they are not things in themselves; they are simply abstracts representing certain qualities of reality.

Let us take the term motion as an example. Mr. Spencer says:

"Here, for instance, is a ship which, for simplicity's sake, we will suppose to be anchored at the equator with her head to the West. When the captain walks from stem to stern, in what direction does he move? East, is the obvious answer,—an answer which for the moment may pass without criticism. But now the anchor is heaved, and the vessel sails to the West with a velocity equal to that at which the captain walks. In what direction does he now move when he goes from stem to stern? You cannot say East, for the vessel is carrying him as fast towards the West as he walks to the East; and you cannot say West for the converse reason. In respect to surrounding space he is stationary; though to all on board the ship he seems to be moving. But now are we quite sure of this conclusion?—Is he really stationary? When we take into account the earth's motion round its axis, we find that instead of being stationary he is travelling at the rate of 1000 miles per hour to the East; so that neither the perception of one who looks at him, nor the inference of one who allows for the ship's motion, is anything like the truth. Nor indeed, on further consideration, shall we find this revised conclusion to be much better. For we have forgotten to allow for the Earth's motion in its orbit. This being some 68,000 miles per hour, it follows that, assuming the time to be midday, he is moving, not at the rate of 1000 miles per hour to the East, but at the rate of 67,000 miles per hour to the West. Nay, not even now have we discovered the true rate and the true direction of his movement. With the Earth's progress in its orbit, we have to join that of the whole Solar system towards the constellation Hercules; and when we do this, we perceive that he is moving neither East nor West, but in a line inclined to the plane of the Ecliptic, and at a velocity greater or less (according to the time of the year) than that above named. To which let us add, that were the dynamic arrangements of our sideral system fully known to us, we should probably discover the direction and rate of his actual movement to differ considerably even from these. How illusive are our ideas of motion, is thus made sufficiently manifest. That which seems moving proves to be stationary; that which seems stationary proves to be moving; while that which we conclude to be going rapidly in one direction, turns out to be going much more rapidly in the opposite direction. And so we are taught that what we are conscious of is not the real motion of any object, either in its rate or direction; but merely its motion as measured from an assigned position—either the position we ourselves occupy or some other."

Motion is a change of place, but this change of place is not something absolute. It is nothing in itself. It is relative and can be determined only by a point of reference. If we omit this reference-point in our description of a certain motion we shall find ourselves unable to determine either its velocity or its direction, and in this way truly "our ideas of motion" are "thus made illusive." To describe a relation without considering it as a relation is nonsensical and must be productive of confusion.

Let us take one more instance. Mr. Spencer says that "all hypotheses respecting the constitution of matter commit us to inconceivable conclusions when logically developed." Now it is a trite truism that we know little of the constitution of the elements, and there are innumerable problems of physics and chemistry unsolved as yet, and our scientists have no hope of solving all these problems within any reasonable time. If this were Mr. Spencer's meaning, we should need no agnosticism to be told so, for the world has known this long ago. Yet this is not Mr. Spencer's meaning. He declares that "matter in its ultimate nature is as absolutely incomprehensible as Space and Time." And the efforts which he makes with the foredetermined aim that they should fail and end in contradictions, are upon the whole attempts to think of matter, force, motion, space, and time, not as abstracts, but as absolute entitities, as things in themselves. They become inconceivable, not by being logically, but by being illogically developed. He says for instance (p. 53):

"The idea of resistance cannot be separated in thought from the idea of an extended body which offers resistance. To suppose that central forces can reside in points not infinitesimally small but occupying no space whatever—points having position only, with nothing to mark their position—points in no respect distinguishable from the surrounding points that are not centres of force;—to suppose this, is utterly beyond human power."

If we suppose that centres of force exist as mathematical points separated from extended bodies, we forget that our ideas of force and of bodies and of extension are mere abstractions. To think of our abstract ideas as if they were things in themselves, absolute existences, will always and necessarily lead us into contradictions.

Things in themselves do not exist; they are ghosts. If we try to conceive the nature of ghosts, we shall naturally turn agnostics, but if we bear in mind that our ideas have been abstracted from reality, that they are symbols describing certain parts or features of reality, we shall soon learn to understand that these ghosts do not exist.

It would lead us too far here to show that Mr. Spencer's method of making every one of "the ultimate scientific ideas" mysterious is throughout the same. He tacitly neglects some of their fundamental features and upon the whole treats them as if they ought to be things in themselves. This method of dealing with the problems of space, time, matter, and motion will strongly appeal to mystic minds, but it will not further our insight. The aim of philosophy is not to confound our concepts, not to entangle our minds in hopeless confusion, but to clarify our ideas and render them precise so that we shall know what they represent and how to employ them.

Philosophy ought to be a clarification of the fundamental conceptions of science; it ought to be the science of science and come to the assistance of all the special sciences by helping them to become conscious of the methods of scientific inquiry; it ought further to teach the specialist to see the interconnexion between all the branches of knowledge and systematise these results into a consistent system; but agnosticism acts like a fog superadding to the things that are known the imaginary quantity, not of the unknown or not yet known, but of the unknowable. And this fog is impenetrable; for Mr. Spencer declares times and again that nothing can be surer than this that the mystery is absolute is inscrutable and transcendent.

If we bear in mind what reality is and what knowledge means, we shall at once understand that anything absolutely unknowable must be non-existent. Whatever exists manifests its existence by affecting other existences. Reality is *Wirklichkeit*, viz., that which works, or manifests itself in effects. Knowledge, however, means representation; whatever affects sensation, either directly or indirectly, can be represented in thought, and whatever can be represented in thought is describable, i. e., knowable.

That knowledge is relative, depending upon the relation between subject and object, renders knowledge as little illusory as existence becomes unreal by being subject to causation. Unknowable is only that which does not manifest itself, everything real acts, *alles wirkliche wirkt*, and becomes thereby representable and describable.

Agnosticism has not freed the world from the ghosts of metaphysicism, and cannot conquer the spook of supernaturalism. It has confessedly nothing to do with them: it lets them alone; but the goblins of mysticism lead a safe life in the realm of the unknowable.

* * *

Mr. Spencer's philosophy is a strange mixture of dogmatism with agnosticism. His agnosticism is a veil that covers unproved and unprovable assumptions. Mr. Spencer would free his philosophy of evolution of its main inconsistency if he discarded the term unknowable. Take for instance the following sentence:

> "Those modes of the Unknowable which we call motion heat, light, chemical affinity, etc., are alike transformable into each other, and into those modes of the Unknowable which we distinguish as sensation, emotion, thought."

The principle of economy is most recommendable everywhere, in practical life, in science, and also in matters of style. Would it not be quite an improvement in Mr. Spencer's writings if he dropped throughout the term "Unknowable," confining himself only to statements of that which is known. The same sentence unencumbered with the "Unknowable" would read:

> "Motion, heat, light, chemical affinity, etc., are alike transformable into each other and into sensation, emotion, thought."

Would not this simplify Mr. Spencer's ideas and render his positive propositions more concise?

If everything is unknowable, of course, motion may be as easily converted into emotion as ink into thought, but a little consideration will teach us that the ideas which I write down are not ink and that the psychological changes in the brain which are accompanied with feelings are not themselves and as such sensations. No psychologist to-day, not even, perhaps the most rabid anti-supernaturalist, would allow Mr. Spencer's dogmatic statement to go unchallenged.

*
* *

The importance which Mr. Spencer attributes to the Unknowable in his theoretical world-conception ought to give it a prominent place also in his ethics, for ethics is nothing but the practical application of a theory. His philosophy is not a unitary and consistent system, but an amalgamation of several incompatible systems. A consistent ethics of agnosticism would be mysticism, i. e., a theory which holds that we feel impelled to do our duty without being able to explain the nature of duty; what conscience, justice, morality, etc., really are, Mr. Spencer ought to say, can never be known. A consistent ethics of the philosophy of evolution would be evolutionism, i. e., the proposition "good is that which enhances the process of evolution, bad is that which hinders it or prepares a dissolution." Mr. Spencer neglects his theories, agnosticism as well as evolutionism, entirely in his ethics, which is a refined Hedonism, and I cannot help considering this as an inconsistency on Mr. Spencer's part.

That Mr. Spencer's philosophy is lacking in more than one respect in consistency is a truth unknown only to his blind followers; but the fact becomes at once obvious to every one who attempts to condense his views. Ueberweg, for instance, says in his *History of Philosophy* (translated from the fourth German edition by Geo. S. Morris, p. 432) in a synopsis of Mr. Spencer's views about matter and mind, which are declared to be unknowable in *First Principles:*

"As to what matter and mind are, he [Mr. Spencer] replies sometimes that we can know it, because a being is required to manifest phenomena, sometimes because persistence in consciousness supposes correspondence in permanent forces, sometimes because the two conceptions are the same, sometimes that matter and mind are simply bundles or series of phenomena and nothing besides. Sometimes he reasons as though causality were a direct and self-evident relation, and sometimes as though this relation were nothing more than an order of sensations and our belief in it were the growth of inseparable associations."

Ueberweg sums up his review of Mr. Spencer in the following paragraph:

"The system of Spencer is still under criticism, and perhaps may not have been fully expounded by its author. Possibly it has not yet been completely developed. Should Spencer continue to devote to philosophy his active energies for many years, it is not inconceivable that new associations may take possession of that physiological organisation which he is accustomed to call himself, and perhaps be evolved under another system of first principles which may displace those which he taught hitherto."

* * *

Mr. Spencer has also tried to reconcile science and religion, and he does it on the basis of the Unknowable. The Unknowable is very convenient for every sleight-of-hand trick, and would lend itself as easily to the reconciliation of Reason and Absurdity.

The first chapter of the *First Principles* (p. 46) ends with the following sentences:

"And thus the mystery which all religions recognise turns out to be a far more transcendent mystery than any of them suspect, —not a relative, but *an absolute mystery.**

"Here, then, is an ultimate religious truth of the highest possible certainty [!]—a truth in which religions in general are at one with each other and with a philosophy antagonistic to their special dogmas. And this truth, respecting which there is a latent agreement among all mankind from the fetish-worshipper to the most stoical critic of human creeds, must be the one we seek. If Re-

*Italics are ours.

ligion and Science are to be reconciled, the basis of reconciliation must be this deepest, widest, and most certain [!] of all facts—that the Power of which the Universe manifests to us is *utterly inscrutable*."*

Mr. Spencer's reconciliation of religion and science on the basis of the Unknowable appears to us very unsatisfactory; and it will be seen to be impracticable because it rests upon erroneous premises. It is not true that on the one side religion is based upon the unknown or unknowable, and on the other side that the ultimate ideas of science are inscrutable and representative of realities that cannot be comprehended.

Religion is everywhere based upon the known and knowable. The savage worships the thunderstorm, not because it is something inscrutable to him, but *because he is afraid of it;* he actually *knows* that it can do him harm. The obvious danger connected with a phenomenon makes man anxious to adapt his conduct to it, so that he will escape unscathed.

If a phenomenon (lightning, dreams, pangs of conscience) is not sufficiently known in its causes, this will breed erroneous conceptions or superstitions, i. e. false religion; and there is no conciliation possible between the latter and science. It is true that the facts of nature which have made man religious were misunderstood by the savage, and most facts are still little understood by the scientists to-day. But it is not this lack of comprehension upon which religion was then and is now based; on the contrary, religion is based upon the more or less clearly conceived idea that we have to conform to a power stronger than we ourselves. There is an authority above all human authority; it is in science the authority of truth, in

* Italics are ours.

the domain of practical life the authority of right, and this authority is not personal but superpersonal. The reconciliation of religion with science, as we understand it, can be brought about only by a purification of our conception of the authority to which we have to submit. That religion will be the purest and highest which holds forth the simple statement of provable truth as the basis of ethics; and this religion cannot be in conflict with science, for it is to be based upon that which we know, and not upon that which we do not know. If a religion, based upon that which we do not know, be found to be reconcilable with science, it will be mere hap-hazard, a matter of pure chance, and at any rate the principle of such a religion will under all circumstances be antagonistic to science.

The actual fact is that a partial knowledge of certain natural phenomena (frequently wrong, sometimes right, at least in its practical application) is the basis of religious action.

Religion asserts itself as an instinct; in its higher stage it is refined into conscience, and in its further growth is destined to become more and more scientific. But even con-*science*, though instinctive and sometimes unclear, is not nescience, but (as the word indicates) a budding "science,"—a knowledge of good and evil growing secretly, in the realm of subliminal soul-life, as the moral instinct of man.

On the one hand, religion is not based upon the unknown; and on the other hand, the ultimate scientific ideas are not incomprehensible.

Monists consider the positive element of knowledge the main thing, while Mr. Spencer on the contrary eliminates the positive element of knowledge and retains the negative element of ignorance, the quintessence of which he calls "the Unknowable,"—oblivious of the fact that in reality there are no such things as negative magnitudes. While Monism leads to the formulation of a Religion of Science, Mr. Spencer proposes a philosophy of nescience, and his conception of religion is the acquiescence in the assumption of an Unknowable. Our conception of God is the recognition of that superpersonal power to which we have to conform, and our knowledge of it increases with the progress of science, while Mr. Spencer's idea of God is the inscrutable mystery which has no reality in the objective world, but exists in his imagination only.

It is just as erroneous for a philosopher to extract that which we do not know as the quintessence of religious belief, as it would be for a chemist to extract all those substances of a body which it does not contain and to consider them as the real thing.

The negative magnitude of the not-yet known is, as all mere possibilities must be, infinite. If this negative magnitude were indeed a positive existence and the essential thing in religion, it would dwarf all progress into insignificance and would stamp upon all our aspirations the curse of vanity.

Mr. Spencer's proposition of the Reconciliation of Science with religion is the assurance that science will leave always an unbounded territory for all kinds of unwarranted assumptions and superstitions, while our proposition implies the purification of religion from erroneous notions. It is the proposition of a great work to be accomplished.

* * *

Philosophy is not mere theory, it is of practical importance. Being the expression of our conception of the world, it determines, perhaps slowly but decisively and unfailingly, our attitude in life. Spencerianism, that is to say, a dilettantism in philosophy, has saturated our intellectual atmosphere and is apt to make our growing generation, our students at the universities and our young professional men, including our theologians who heretofore have been Mr. Spencer's enemies, superficial and satisfied with negations.

Agnostic stock phrases, unmeaning though they are, fill the air and are accepted as axioms, poisoning philosophy, science, psychology, and ethics. We are told that "the finite cannot comprehend the infinite;"* that the ultimate nature of matter and motion† is an inscrutable mystery; that "the substance of the mind remains forever unknown;"‡ that ethics means "the greatest happiness of the greatest number;"§ and generalisation|| is praised as the highest accomplishment of the human mind, no use being made of discrimination, which is the more important and at the same time rarer faculty of mind which distinguishes the man of science.¶

* See *Fundamental Problems*, p. 161 ff., p. 169 ff., p. 287 ff; the "Salutatory" in the January number of *The Open Court*, 1897, p. 9; and *Homilies of Science*, pp. 108-111. Cf. p. 55 of the present booklet.

† The terms matter and motion are the most general terms of their kind. The idea of matter is not more mysterious than "lead, copper, zinc, wood," etc., but simpler and less mysterious.

‡ Mind is spiritual and does not consist of substances of any kind. We may inquire into the nature of mind but the very phrase "substance of mind" is a self-stultification and starts the investigator in the wrong direction.

§ For a treatment of this problem in humorous form see the author's tale "The Philosopher's Martyrdom," in *Truth in Fiction*. (Chicago, 1893).

|| See *Fundamental Problems*, pp, 101 ff.

¶ This article is not intended to exhaust the subject, and the reader is referred to other essays of the author, *The Primer of Philosophy*, the article "Are There Things in Themselves?" in *The Monist*, Vol. II, No. 2, p. 225.

We cannot here discuss all these questions as they deserve, and repeat only what we have stated on former occasions, that agnosticism as an *attitude* is praiseworthy, but as a *doctrine* objectionable.

If we understand by agnosticism that, before we have good reasons to say, we know a certain thing, we must suspend our judgment, it is highly recommendable. If a confession of ignorance is to be called agnosticism, it is the agnosticism of modesty; and there is no one, be he ever so wise and learned, who would not in a great many fields have to own that he is an agnostic.

But the case is at once changed if a man argues that because he does not know, no one can know. He makes of agnosticism a doctrine, and the modesty of his declaration of ignorance is transformed into arrogance. The agnosticism of modesty is the beginning of wisdom, but the agnosticism of arrogance is the worst kind of dogmatism; it is illiberal because it declares that no one else can have anything to say worth listening to; it is reactionary because it prevents investigation and stops progress; it is antiscientific because if its premises are true a sage knows as little as a fool; it is unphilosophical because instead of proposing a solution of the main problems of existence it declares them to be insolvable and thus may be called a declaration of philosophical bankruptcy. In fine, we re ject agnosticism as a philosophy unfit for adoption and even dangerous if taken seriously.

It is a matter of course that in rejecting Mr. Spencer's agnosticism we do not mean to say that it did not serve a good purpose as a transitional phase.

Mr. Spencer appeared at a juncture when a philosophy was needed that remained on the surface and indulged in glittering generalities. His dogmatism is well adapted to those who had just freed themselves from the yoke of creeds. Thus he became the recognised apostle of the last half century, first among the broad middle classes of North America who were hungry for some philosophy which would be intelligible and then also in his own country. But the time has now come, when the people demand solid food instead of husks. Mr. Spencer's authority is waning and he remains the oracle of progressive thought only among those classes who lack critical acumen.

The rise of Mr. Spencer's fame is as natural as its decline.

His place in the history of philosophy is that of an awakener from traditionalism. He made the people doubt and roused a philosophical interest in large masses who were heretofore indifferent to philosophic thought and perhaps entirely unable to think for themselves. While Mr. Spencer's purely negative doctrine will prove to be very shortlived, not having roots to give it strength, the impetus which he gave to rational enquiry will be ineradicably lasting even when the present generation, and with it the need that gave currency to his agnosticism, has long long passed away.

MR. SPENCER'S COMMENT AND THE AUTHOR'S REPLY.

MR. HERBERT SPENCER in a republication of his essay: *The Ethics of Kant* together with many other older articles in a work of three volumes entitled *Essays Scientific, Political, and Speculative*, 1891, repeats the following sentence:

"Thus the basis of the argument by which Kant attempts to justify his assumption that there exists a good will apart from a good end, disappears utterly; and leaves his dogma in all its naked unthinkableness."

To this sentence he adds in a foot-note a comment on my criticisms, which is here reproduced.

MR. SPENCER'S COMMENT.

"I find that in the above three paragraphs I have done Kant less than justice and more than justice—less, in assuming that his evolutionary view was limited to the genesis of our sidereal system, and more, in assuming that he had not contradicted himself. My knowledge of Kant's writings is extremely limited. In 1844 a translation of his 'Critique of Pure Reason' (then I think lately published) fell into my hands, and I read the first few pages enunciating his doctrine of Time and Space: my peremptory rejection of which caused me to lay the book down. Twice since then the same thing has happened; for, being an impatient reader, when I disagree with the cardinal propositions of a work I can go no further. One other thing I knew. By indirect references I was made aware that Kant had propounded the idea that celestial bodies have been formed by the aggregation of diffused matter. Beyond this my knowledge of his conceptions did not extend; and my supposition that his evolutionary conception had stopped short with the genesis of sun, stars, and planets, was due to the fact that his doctrine of Time and Space, as forms of thought anteceding experience, implied a supernatural origin inconsistent with the hypothesis of natural genesis. Dr. Paul Carus, who, shortly after the publication of this article in the *Fortnightly Review* for July, 1888, undertook to defend the Kantian ethics in the American journal which he edits, *The Open Court*, has now (Sept. 4, 1890), in another defensive article, translated sundry passages from Kant's 'Critique of Judgment,' his 'Presumable Origin of Humanity,' and his work 'Upon the different Races of Mankind,' showing that Kant was, if not fully, yet partially, an evolutionist in his speculations about living beings. There is, perhaps, some reason for doubting the correctness of Dr. Carus's rendering of these passages into English. When, as in the first of the articles just named, he failed to distinguish between consciousness and conscientiousness, and when, as in this last article, he blames the English for mistranslating Kant, since they have said 'Kant maintained that Space and Time are intuitions,' which is quite untrue, for they have everywhere described him as maintaining that Space and Time are *forms* of intuition, one may be excused for thinking that possibly Dr. Carus has read into some of Kant's expressions, meanings which they do not rightly bear. Still, the general drift of the passages quoted makes it tolerably clear that Kant must have believed in the operation of natural causes as largely, though not entirely, instrumental in producing organic forms: extending this belief (which he says 'can be named a daring venture of reason') in some measure to the origin of Man himself. He does not, however, extend the theory of natural genesis to the exclusion of the theory of supernatural genesis. When he speaks of an organic habit 'which in the wisdom of nature appears to be thus arranged in order that the species shall be preserved'; and when, further, he says 'we see, moreover, that a germ of reason is placed in him, whereby, after the development of the same, he is destined for social intercourse,' he implies divine intervention. And this shows that I was justified in ascribing to him the belief that Space and Time, as forms of thought, are supernatural endowments. Had he conceived of organic evolution in a consistent manner, he would necessarily have regarded Space and Time as subjective forms generated by converse with objective realities.

"Beyond showing that Kant had a partial, if not a complete, belief in organic evolution (though with no idea of its causes), the passages translated by Dr. Carus show that he entertained an implied belief which it here specially concerns me to notice as bearing on his theory of 'a good will.' He quotes approvingly Dr. Moscati's lecture showing 'that the upright walk of man is constrained and unnatural,' and showing the imperfect visceral arrangements and consequent diseases which result: not only adopting, but further illustrating, Dr. Moscati's argument. If here, then, there is a distinct admission, or rather assertion, that various human organs are imperfectly adjusted to their functions, what becomes of the postulate above quoted 'that no organ for any purpose will be found in it but what is also the fittest and best adapted for that purpose'? And what becomes of the argument which sets out with this postulate? Clearly, I am indebted to Dr. Carus for enabling me to prove that Kant's defence of his theory of 'a good will' is, by his own showing, baseless."

REPLY TO MR. SPENCER.

Mr. Spencer's comments on my criticisms are surprising in more than one respect.

First, without even mentioning the objections I make he discredits my arguments by throwing doubt upon the correctness of the translations of the quoted passages.

Secondly, he alleges, with a view of justifying his doubt, that in the first of my articles I "failed to distinguish between consciousness and conscientiousness."

Thirdly, Mr. Spencer declares that I had "read into some of Kant's expressions, meanings which they do not rightly bear."

Fourthly, Mr. Spencer bases this opinion upon a double mistake: he blames me for not distinguishing between the Kantian phrases that "Space and Time are intuitions" and that they are "forms of intuition."

Fifthly, acknowledging after all that Kant had at least "a partial belief in organic evolution," Mr. Spencer accuses him of inconsistency.

Sixthly, several statements concerning Kant's views are made not because Kant held them but because Mr. Spencer assumes for trivial reasons that he is "justified in ascribing them to him."

Seventhly, these statements so vigorously set forth are accompanied by Mr. Spencer's remarkably frank confession of unfamiliarity with the subject under discussion.

It may be added that Mr. Spencer calls my criticisms "defensive articles." He says that I "undertook to defend the Kantian ethics"; while in fact, my articles are aggressive. Kant needs no defence for being misunderstood, and it would not be my business to defend him, for I am not a Kantian in the sense that I adopt any of the main doctrines of Kant. On the contrary I dissent from him on almost all fundamental questions. In ethics I object to Kant's views in so far as they can be considered as pure formalism.* I am a Kantian only in the sense that I respect Kant as one of the most eminent philosophers, that I revere him as that teacher of mine whose influence upon me was greatest, and I consider the study of Kant's works as an indispensable requisite for understanding the problems of the philosophy of our time. Far from defending Kant's position, I only undertook to inform Mr. Spencer of what Kant had really maintained, so that instead of denouncing absurdities which Kant had never thought of, he might criticise the real Kant.

*
* *

What does *Anschauung* mean? No one can understand Kant who misconceives Kant's use of the term *Anschauung*. The subject is of great importance and Mr. Spencer's erroneous statement that Kant conceives space and time as forms of thought instead of forms of intuition induces me to make a few explanatory remarks concerning the term *Anschauung*.

*See *Fundamental Problems*, pp. 197–206; and *The Ethical Problem*, p. 32, et seq., especially p. 33, lines 18–20.

Kant means that space and time are immediately given in experience and not inferences drawn from the data of experience; they are not thoughts, but objects of direct perception.

Sense-impressions are data, they are prior to ideas, the latter being constructions made out of sense-impressions. Sense-impressions are facts, but ideas are of an inferential nature; they are (to use Lloyd Morgan's excellent term) constructs. Now Kant claims that space and time are in the same predicament as the resistance of material objects. They are not objects, they are mere forms; but like objects, they are immediately given, they belong to *Anschauung*.

Kant was very careful on the one hand to show that time and space are mere forms and not objects or essences and on the other hand that they are not ideas, not thoughts, not abstractions, not generalisations, but that they are as direct data as are sense-impressions and he calls the knowledge which man has by directly facing the object of knowledge "*Anschauung.*"

The conclusion which Kant draws from this may be characterised as follows:

Sensations are not things but appearances; they are subjective, not objective, they are not the objects themselves but what our sensibility makes of objects. Space and time being *Anschauungen,* Kant argues that they are of the same kind as the sense-data of knowledge, that they are inherent in our nature. Thus Kant maintains: "Sensations are the products of our sensibility, and space and time are the forms of our sensibility."

The word *Anschauung* has been a *crux interpretum* since translations have been made from Kant, and it is quite true that no adequate word to express it exists in English.

The Journal of Speculative Philosophy contains several notes on this mooted subject. The following is from the pen of Dr. W. T. Harris (Vol. II, p. 191):

"Through a singular chance, the present number of the Journal contains two notes from two contributors on the proper translation of the German word *Anschauung*. Mr. Kroeger holds that the word *Anschauung*, as used by Fichte and also by Kant, denotes an act of the Ego which the English word *intuition* does not at all express, but for which the English word 'contemplation is an exact equivalent. Mr. Peirce suggests that no person whose native tongue is English will translate *Anschauung* by another word than *intuition*. Whether there is a failure to understand English on the one hand or German on the other, the Editor does not care to inquire. It is certain that while intuition has been adopted generally as an equivalent for the word under consideration both by English and French translators, yet it was a wide departure from the ordinary English use of the term. Besides this, we have no English verb *intuite* (at least in the dictionaries), and the reader will find that the verb used by Meiklejohn (in the translation of Kant's *Kritik*) for it, is *contemplate*, and the same rendering is given by Smith in his excellent translation of Fichte's *Popular Works* (London, 1849)."

Mr. Charles S. Peirce says:

"No person whose native tongue is English will need to be informed that contemplation is essentially (1) protracted (2) voluntary, and (3) an action, and that it is never used for that which is set forth to the mind in this act. A foreigner can convince himself of this by the proper study of English writers. Thus, Locke (*Essay concerning Human Understanding*, Book II., chap. 19, § 1) says, 'If it [an idea] be held there [in view] long under attentiv- consideration, 'tis *contemplation*'; and again, (*Ibid.*, Book II., chap. 10, § 1) 'Keeping the *Idea*, which is brought into it [the mind] for some time actually in view, which is called *Contemplation*.' This term is therefore unfitted to translate *Anschauung*; for this latter does not imply an act which is necessarily protracted or voluntary, and denotes most usually a mental presentation, sometimes a faculty, less often the reception of an impression in the mind, and seldom, if ever, an action.

"To the translation of *Anschauung* by *intuition*, there is, at least, no such insufferable objection. Etymologically the two words precisely correspond. The original philosophical meaning of intuition was a cognition of the present manifold in that character; and it is now commonly used, as a modern writer says, 'to include all the products of the perceptive (external or internal) and imagine ative faculties; every act of consciousness, in short, of which the immediate object is an *individual*, thing, act, or state of mind, presented under the condition of distinct existence in space and time.' Finally, we have the authority of Kant's own example for translating his *Anschauung* by *Intuitus;* and, indeed, this is the common usage of Germans writing Latin. Moreover, *intuitiv* frequently replaces *anschauend* or *anschaulich*. If this constitutes a misunderstanding of Kant, it is one which is shared by himself and nearly all his countrymen" (*ibid.* p. 152 et seqq.)

Mr. Peirce adds the following explanation concerning the term *intuition* in another note (*ibid.* p. 103):

"The word *intuitus* first occurs as a technical term in St. Anselm's Monologium. He wished to distinguish between our knowledge of God and our knowledge of finite things (and, in the next world, of God, also); and thinking of the saying of St. Paul, *Videmus nunc per speculum in ænigmate; tunc autem facie ad faciem*, he called the former *speculation* and the latter *intuition* This use of 'speculation' did not take root, because that word already had another exact and widely different meaning.

"In the middle ages, the term 'intuitive cognition' had two principal senses, 1st, as opposed to abstractive cognition, it meant the knowledge of the present as present, and this is its meaning in Anselm; but 2d, as no intuitive cognition was allowed to be determined by a previous cognition, it came to be used as the opposite of discursive cognition (see Scotus, In sentent. lib. 2, dist. 3, qu. 9), and this is nearly the sense in which I employ it. This is also nearly the sense in which Kant uses it, the former distinction being expressed by his *sensuous* and *non-sensuous*. (See Werke, herausg. Rosenkrantz, Thl. 2, S. 713, 31, 41, 100 u. s. w.)

"An enumeration of six meanings of intuition may be found in Hamilton's Reid p. 759."

If we have to choose between the two translations *intuition* and *contemplation*, we should with Mr. Peirce decidedly prefer the word *intuition*. The word *contemplation* corresponds to the German *Betrachtung* and all that Mr. Peirce says against it holds good. But we must confess that the term *intuition* (as Mr. Peirce himself seems to grant) is not a very good translation either. The term *intuition* has other meanings which interfere with the correct meaning of *Anschauung* and was actually productive of much confusion.

The English term *intuition* is strongly tinged with the same meaning that is attached to the German word *Intuition*. It means an inexplicable kind of direct information from some supernatural source, which mystics claim to possess as the means of their revelations. In this sense Goethe characterises it satirically in Faust (Scene XIV). Mephistopheles describes the process as follows:

> "A blessing drawn from supernatural fountains!
> In night and dew to lie upon the mountains;
> All Heaven and Earth in rapture penetrating;
> Thyself to Godhood haughtily inflating;
> To grub with yearning force through Earth's dark marrow,
> Compress the six days' work within thy bosom narrow,—
> To taste, I know not what, in haughty power,
> Thine own ecstatic life on all things shower,
> Thine earthly self behind thee cast,
> And then the lofty intuition [with a gesture] at last."

The satire is good on *Intuition* but it would not apply to *Anschauung*, for the latter word excludes rigidly any mysticism or supernaturalism which the former essentially involves. To employ the term "intuition" for both ideas must necessarily weaken the meaning of *Anschauung*.

Besides we should bear in mind that the German *Anschauung* is vernacular and should find a corresponding Saxon word. Such Latin words as *intuition* convey in English as much as in German the impres sion of being terms denoting something very abstract. Vernacular terms much more strongly indicate the immediateness and directness which is implied in *Anschauung*. In a conversation with Mr. F. C. Russell, a lawyer of Chicago, interested in philosophy, we tried to coin a new word that should cover the meaning of *Anschauung* as an act of "atlooking," and the word "atsight" readily suggested itself.

The word "atsight" is an exact English equivalent of the German *Anschauung*. It describes the looking at an object in its immediate presence. At the same time the word is readily understood, while philologically considered, its formation is fully justified by the existence of the words "insight and foresight."

* * *

One of the most important of Kant's doctrines is the proposition that all thought must ultimately have reference to *Anschauung*, i. e. to atsight. Through atsight only the objects of experience can be given us. All speculations not founded upon this bottom rock of knowledge are mere dreams. This is the maxim of positivism and it is the basis of all sound philosophy. Says Kant in the "Anhang" to his *Prolegomena* (in reply to a critic who had misunderstood his idealism) as a summary statement of his views :

"*Der Satz aller echten Idealisten, von der eleatischen Schule an bis zum Bischof Berkeley, ist in dieser Formel enthalten. 'alles Erkenntnis durch Sinne und Erfahrung ist nichts als lauter Schein, und nur in den Ideen des reinen Verstandes und der Vernunft ist Wahrheit.'*

"*Der Grundsatz, der meinen Idealismus durchgängig regiert und bestimmt, ist dagegen: 'Alles Erkenntnis von Dingen, aus blossem reinen Verstande oder reiner Vernunft, ist nichts als lauter Schein, und nur in der Erfahrung ist Wahrheit.*'"

"The doctrine of all genuine idealists from the Eleatic School down to Bishop Berkeley is contained in this formula: All cognition through the senses and experience is nothing but illusion; and in the ideas of the pure understanding and reason alone is truth.

"The principle, however, that rules and determines my idealism throughout is this: All cognition out of pure understanding or pure reason is nothing but mere illusion and in experience alone is truth."

Kant then proposes in order to avoid equivocation to call his views "formal or critical idealism," adding that his idealism made any other idealism impossible. Criticism truly is the beginning of philosophy as an objective science. It gives the *coup de grace* to those worthless declamations which still pass among many as philosophy. Says Kant:

"*So viel ist gewiss: wer einmal Kritik gekostet hat, den ekelt auf immer alles dogmatische Gewäsche.*"

"That much is certain: He who has once tasted critique will be forever disgusted with all dogmatic twaddle."

It is strange that in spite of Kant's explicit declaration, which leaves no doubt about the positive spirit that pervades the principles of his philosophy, he is still misunderstood by his opponents and frequently no less by those who profess to be his disciples.

* * *

There is no occasion now to treat the subject exhaustively, but it may be permitted to add a few remarks on Kant's proposition that space and time are atsights.

We must distinguish three things:

1) Objective space.

2) Space as atsight, and

3) Space-conception.

Space as atsight is the datum. It is the immediate presence of relations among the sensory impressions. This, however, is not as yet that something which we generally call space. That which generally goes by the name of space is a construction built out of the relational data that obtain in experience and we propose to call it space-conception. Our space-conception, accordingly, (and here I include the mathematician's space-conception) is based upon space as atsight, but it is more than atsight. It is an inference made therefrom, it is the product of experience. Space-conception, however, is, as are all legitimate noumena, no mere subjective illusion, it possesses objective validity, it describes some real existence and this real existence represented in space-conception is what may be called objective space.

Objective space is the form of reality. Space as atsight is the form of sensibility. Space as space-conception is a construct of an abstract nature and serves as a description or plan of the form of reality.

The same is true of Time. Time as atsight is the relation of succession obtaining in the changes of experience. Time as time-conception is the noumenon constructed out of these data to describe and determine the succession of events, that feature of reality which may be called objective time.

Briefly: Space and Time are not things, not essences, not entities, but certain features of existence. They are the forms of reality. When existence finds a representation in the feelings of a sentient being, time and space appear as their forms, and these forms furnish the material out of which are built the conceptions of Space and Time.

* * *

It appears that Mr. Spencer for some strange reasons, which seem to be based upon mere prepossession, is incapable of grasping Kant's meaning and the significance of his terms. Not minding the purport of Kant's investigation, Mr. Spencer knows nothing of the significance of the contrast made in the *Critique of Pure Reason* between *Anschauung* (intuition or "atsight," i. e., the direct and concrete data of perception) and *Denken* (thought, i. e., the abstractions and generalisations made from these data), and he censured Kant in the first edition of his *Principles of Psychology* for calling Space and Time "forms of thought" and attributing them to the ego. Kantians called Mr. Spencer's attention to the fact that Space and Time according to Kant are "forms of intuition" not "forms of thought," and so Mr. Spencer proceeds to replace in the second edition the term "forms of thought" by "forms of intuition," but he claims that some Kantians have used the phrase "forms of thought" and adds that "relatively to the question at issue, whether Time and Space belong to the *ego* or the *non-ego*, the distinction is wholly unimportant, and indeed irrelevant."

Here are Mr. Spencer's own words:

"Throughout this discussion I use the expression "forms of intuition," and avoid the expression "forms of thought," which I used in the first edition of this work; and for using which I have, along with other writers, been blamed. In the course of a controversy carried on in *Nature*, from January 3 to February 10th, 1870, it was pointed out by Mr. Lewes, who was one of those charged with this misrepresentation, that among others who have used the phrase "forms of thought" to express this doctrine of Kant, are sundry professed Kantists, as Dr. Whewell and Sir W. Hamilton (a great stickler for precision); and he might have added to these, Dr. Mansel, who is also an exact writer, not likely to have misapprehended or misstated his master's meaning. The fact is that, relatively to the question at issue, whether Time and Space belong to the *ego* or to the *non-ego*, the distinction is wholly unimportant, and indeed irrelevant. If some one were to quote the statement of a certain chemist, to the effect that broadcloth is a nitrogenous substance; and if another were to contradict him, saying—no, his statement is that wool is a nitrogenous substance; the objection would, I think, be held frivolous, when the question in dispute was whether the matter of wool contains nitrogen or not. And I do not see much more pertinence in the objection that Kant called Time and Space "forms of intuition" (raw material of thought), and not "forms of thought" itself (in which the raw material is woven together); when the thing contended is, that Time and Space belong neither to woven thought nor to its unwoven materials."

Mr. Spencer apparently believes that according to Kant, Space and Time have no application in the world of objects (i. e., the *non-ego*).*

* Kant never said that Space and Time belonged to the *ego* and not to the *non-ego*, he claims that they are ideal. they are forms of *Anschauung*. Kant's mode of reasoning indeed suggests the idea that he would attribute them to the *ego* and preclude them from the *non-ego*. But when criticising an author, we ought to use his expressions and condemn his mistakes in his own words. Mr. Spencer has no right to substitute his own language for Kant's. It is like pronouncing a verdict without allowing the defendant to plead his case, but to have it pleaded by the state's attorney, who like the judge represents the prosecuting party. I do not agree with Kant's conception of Time and Space, but I claim that his views if stated in his own language are not so senseless and idiotic as they appear in Mr. Spencer's recapitulation dressed up by Mr. Spencer for the special purpose of overthrowing them. Kant says for instance in § 3 under the caption *Schlüsse* second Paragraph: "Der Raum ist nichts anderes als nur die Form aller Erscheinungen äusserer Sinne," and further down: Unsere Erörterungen lehren demnach die Realität (d. i. objective Giltigkeit) des Raumes in Ansehung alles dessen, was äusserlich als Gegenstand uns vorkommen kann, aber zugleich die Idealität des Raumes in Ansehung der Dinge, wenn sie durch die Vernunft an sich selbst erwogen werden, d. i. ohne Rücksicht auf die Beschaffenheit unserer Sinnlichkeit zu nehmen. Wir behaupten also die empirische Realität des Raumes (in Ansehung aller mög-

Professor Sylvester one of Mr. Spencer's critics said of Mr. Spencer's misinterpretation of Kant:

"It is clear that if Mr. Spencer had been made aware of the broad line of demarcation in Kant's system between Intuition, the action or the product of the Sensibility, and Thought, the action or product of the Understanding (the two belonging, according to Kant, to entirely different provinces of the mind), he would have seen that his supposed refutation proceeded on a mere misapprehension of Kant's actual utterance and doctrine on the subject. If Mr. Spencer will restore to Kant the words really used by him, the sentence will run thus:—'If space and time are forms of intuition, they can never be thought of; since it is impossible for anything to be at once the *form* of thought and the *matter* of thought;' and his epigram (for Mr. Spencer must have meant it rather as an epigram than as a serious argument) loses all its point. Was it *à priori* that Kant (*the* Kant) should have laid himself open to such a *scholar's mate* at the very outset of his system?"

How little Mr. Spencer is capable of catching the sense of either Kant or Professor Sylvester's criticism appears from the reply which he makes. He says:

"I have only to remark that Professor Sylvester's mode of rendering my criticism pointless, is a very curious, but not, I think, a very conclusive one. He has substituted Kant's words for my words in one part of the sentence quoted (from *First Principles*, p. 49), while he has made no corresponding substitutions in the correlative parts of the sentence. Had he put 'intuition' for 'thought' everywhere, instead of only in one place, my sentence would have run thus: 'If space and time are forms of intuition they can never be intuited; since it is impossible for anything to be at once the *form* of intuition and the *matter* of intuition.'"

Why should space and time, if they are forms of intuition (i. e., Kant's *Anschauung*), never be intuited, i. e., be immediately perceived as atsights, as directly

lichen äusseren Erfahrung)." This does not sound so ridiculous as Mr. Spencer would make us believe. Kant obviously does not deny the objective validity of Space and Time, and most emphatically extends its validity to the *non-ego* (i. e., the objective world).

given data of our perception?* In fact Kant maintains that they are and I do not know of any sane man who would deny the statement if he understands it. Space and Time are the forms of our sensibility, which implies that they belong to concrete phenomena, not to the domain of abstractions. It is true that a thing can not be at the same time form and matter, and so Space and Time can not be at the same time the *form* of intuition and *matter* of intuition. But both matter and form can be perceived or intuited at the same time.

The alteration which Mr. Spencer deems just, if Professor Sylvester's change in one case be allowed, would not save Mr. Spencer's position but only renders his mistake more obvious. His criticism is as meaningless as before, but Mr. Spencer finds not much difference between either renderings, except that he has now brought out the point more clearly. He adds:

> "I fail to see that in the sentence as thus altered the point is lost: if it was there before, it is there now. Indeed, as I think the text shows, the change of expression which Professor Sylvester's objection has led me to make, renders the disproof much clearer than it was before."

What can we expect of a philosopher who is so persistent in perverting the meaning of terms!†

*Mr. Spencer seems to understand "forms of intuition" in the sense of "organs of intuition," and believes that as the eye cannot see itself, so the forms of intuition cannot be intuited; but that is a perversion of the meaning of the term. "To be intuited" is equivalent to the German *angeschaut werden*, and I fail to understand Mr. Spencer's logic why when beholding material objects we should be unable to behold their forms.

† Mr. Spencer claims in his letter, published on page 101 of this book that his "use of the expression forms of thought instead of forms of intuition was simply an inadvertence." We learn from the passages quoted above that Mr. Spencer felt urged by his critics to substitute the latter term for the former one, and that it was, indeed, a mere inadvertence on his part to use the term again; but his claim that the change is indifferent alone proves how little Spencer understood the meaning of his critics. The fact remains that Mr.

I shall now take up the details of Mr. Spencer's reply.

I.

I am sorry to see that Mr. Spencer, instead of frankly acknowledging his errors, has taken refuge in discrediting the translations, which might very easily have been examined either by himself or by friends of his; especially as the German original of the most important passages, wherever any doubt might arise, and also of those expressions on the misconception of which Mr. Spencer bases his unfavorable opinion of Kant, was added in foot-notes.

II.

But Mr. Spencer adduces, as if it were a fact, an instance of my grave mistakes. He says that I failed to distinguish between "consciousness" and "conscientiousness." Mr. Spencer is obviously mistaken; but even if it were as he assumes, we are astonished how much he makes of a small matter, which if as alleged, should be considered as a mere misprint.

Mr. Spencer's statement is so positive that it must make on any reader the impression of being indubitably true. However, in the whole first article of mine, and indeed in both articles, "conscientiousness" is nowhere mentioned and it would be wrong to replace the word "consciousness" in any of the passages in which it occurs by "conscientiousness."

I should be glad if Mr. Spencer would kindly point out to me the passage which he had in mind when making his statement, for since there is not even so much as an occasion for confounding consciousness

Spencer does not criticise Kant (with whose philosophy he is utterly unfamiliar) but a straw man built of his own misconceptions of Kant's philosophy.

and conscientiousness, I stand here before a psychological problem. Mr. Spencer's statement is a perfect riddle to me. Either I have a negative hallucination, as psychologists call it, so that I do not see what is really there, or Mr. Spencer must have had a positive hallucination. That which Mr. Spencer has read into my article, was never written and it is not there. The alleged fact to which he refers, does not exist.

This kind of erroneous reference into which Mr. Spencer has inadvertently fallen is a very grievous mistake. It appears more serious than a simple slip of the pen, when we consider that Mr. Spencer uses the statement for the purpose of incrimination. He justifies upon this exceedingly slender basis his doubt concerning the correctness of the translations of the quoted passages, and Mr. Spencer's doubt concerning the correctness of these translations is his main argument for rejecting my criticisms *in toto*.

It is not impossible, indeed it is probable, that Mr. Spencer meant "conscience" instead of "conscientiousness." We have become accustomed to worse cases of inadvertence in his criticism and censures. There is one passage in which a superficial reader might have expected "conscience" in place of "consciousness." However that does not occur in any of the translations, but in a paragraph where I speak on my own account. This passage appears on page 25, line 14, and in the following sentences. Whatever anybody might have expected in that passage, I certainly intended to say "consciousness," and only a hasty reader, only he who might merely read the first line of the paragraph, would consider the word "consciousness" a mistake.

To avoid any equivocation, however, even to hasty

readers, and to guard against a misconstruction such as Mr. Spencer possibly has given to the sentence, I would be willing to alter the passage by adding a few words as follows:

> "It is quite true that *not only conscience, but* every state of consciousness is a feeling," etc.*

The italicised words are inserted, simply to show that here I mean "consciousness," *not* conscience and *not* conscientiousness. For the rest, they do not alter in the least the sense of the sentence. In this passage as throughout the whole article the terms "consciousness," and "conscience" have been used properly.

* * *

Observing that Mr. Spencer himself appears to have committed the mistake for which he erroneously blames me, I do not mean to say that he "failed to distinguish between" conscientiousness and conscience. I should rather regard it as trifling on my part if I drew this inference from what is either a slip of the pen or an oversight in proof-reading. But it strikes me that that knavish rogue among the fairies whom Shakespeare calls Puck and scientists define as chance or coincidence played in a fit of anger and perhaps from a sentiment of pardonable irony a humorous trick upon Mr. Spencer. The moral of it is that when an author censures his fellow authors with undue severity for things that might be mere misprints, he should keep a close eye on his own printer's devil.

III.

Mr. Spencer discredits my knowledge of Kant. He says of me:

*We have not altered the passage in the present reprint, which remains as Mr. Spencer read it.

"One may be excused for thinking that possibly Dr. Carus has read into some of Kant's expressions, meanings which they do not rightly bear."

I did not give Mr. Spencer any occasion for making this personal reflexion. I do not boast of any extraordinary familiarity with Kant's writings. There are innumerable German and also English and American scholars and philosophers who know Kant almost by heart. But the question at issue is not what I conceive Kant's ideas to be, but what Kant has really said, and I was very careful to let Kant speak for himself.

My criticism of Mr. Spencer's conception of Kant consisted almost exclusively in collating and contrasting Mr. Spencer's views of Kant with quotations from Kant's works. How can I read anything into some of Kant's expressions, if I present translations of the expressions themselves, adding thereto in foot-notes the original whenever doubts could arise? And the general drift of the quotations alone suffices to overthrow Mr. Spencer's conception of Kant.

The truth is that Mr. Spencer himself committed the mistake, for which he censures me unjustly. "Mr. Spencer has read into some of Kant's expressions meanings which they do not rightly bear."

IV.

But Mr. Spencer adduces a fact, which, if it were as Mr. Spencer represents it, would show an inability on my part of making important distinctions. He says of me:

"He blames the English for mistranslating Kant, since they have said 'Kant maintained that Space and Time are intuitions,' which is quite untrue, for they have everywhere described him as maintaining that Space and Time are *forms* of intuitions."

This is a double mistake: (1) Kant and his translators did not make the distinction of which Mr. Spencer speaks, and (2) the quotation Mr. Spencer makes from my article is represented to mean something different from what it actually means in the context.

Before I speak for myself as to what I actually said, let us state the facts concerning Kant's usage of the terms "intuitions" and "forms of intuition."

Kant defines in § 1 of his "Critique of Pure Reason" what he understands by "Transcendental Æsthetic." He distinguishes between "empirical intuition" (*empirische Anschauung*) und "pure intuition" (*reine Anschauung*). He says:

"That sort of intuition which relates to an object by means of sensation, is called an empirical intuition."

Representations contain besides that which belongs to sensation some other elements. Kant says:

"That which effects that the content of the phenomenon can be arranged under certain relations, I call its *forms*."

And later on he continues:

"This pure form of sensibility I shall call pure intuition."

These are Kant's phrases in J. M. D. Meiklejohn's well known translation. The term "pure intuition" is repeated again and again, and we find frequently added by way of explanation the phrases "as a mere form of sensibility," "the mere form of phenomena," "forms of sensuous intuition," and also (as Mr. Spencer emphasises as the only correct way) "forms of intuition."

Kant says:

1) "*Diese reine Form der Sinnlichkeit wird auch selber reine Anschauung heissen.* § 1.

2) "*Zweitens werden wir von dieser (der empirischen Anschauung) noch alles abtrennen, damit nichts als reine Anschauung und die blosse Form der Erscheinungen übrig bleibe.* § 1.

3) "*Raum . . . . muss ursprünglich Anschauung sein.* § 3.

4) "*Der Raum ist nichts anderes als nur die Form aller Erscheinungen äusserer Sinne.* § 3.

5) "*Der Raum aber betrifft nur die reine Form der Anschauung.* (This passage appears in the first edition only, the paragraph containing it is omitted in the second edition. § 3.

6) "*Die Zeit ist . . . . eine reine Form der sinnlichen Anschauung. . . .* § 4.

7) "*Es muss ihr* unmittelbare Anschauung zum Grunde liegen.* § 4.

8) "*Die Zeit ist nichts anderes als die Form des inneren Sinnes.* § 6.

9) "*. . . . dass die Vorstellung der Zeit selbst Anschauung sei.* §6.

10) "*Wir haben nun . . . . reine Anschauung a priori, Raum und Zeit.* § 10. *Beschluss der transcendentalen Æsthetik.*"

These quotations do not pretend to be exhaustive, nor is that necessary for the present purpose.

Kant, as we learn from these quotations, makes no distinction between *reine Anschauung* and *Form der Anschauung.* He uses most frequently the term *reine Anschauung* and designates in several places Space and Time simply as *Anschauung.* (See the quotations 3, 7, and 9.) So far as I can gather from a renewed perusal, the expression proposed by Mr. Spencer, "form of intuition," *Form der Anschauung*, occurs only once and that too in a passage omitted in the second edition.

It is almost redundant to add that the English translators and interpreters of Kant follow the original pretty closely. Accordingly it is actually incorrect

*Second edition reads "*ihnen*" in place of "*ihr*," viz. *der Zeit.* The word "*ihnen*" refers to *Theilvorstellungen der Zeit.*

"that they have everywhere (!) described Kant as maintaining that Space and Time are *forms* of intuition." In addition to the quotations from Meiklejohn, I call Mr. Spencer's attention to William Flemming's "Vocabulary of Philosophy" (4th ed., edited by Henry Calderwood) which reads *sub voce* "Intuition," p. 228 with reference to Kant's view:

> "Space and time are *intuitions* of sense."

To say "Time and Space are forms of intuition" is quite correct according to Kantian terminology. No objection can be made to Mr. Spencer on that ground. But to say "Time and Space are intuitions" is also quite correct, and Mr. Spencer is wrong in censuring the expression.

Why does Mr. Spencer rebuke me so severely on a point which is of no consequence? He appears confident that I have betrayed an unpardonable misconception of Kant's philosophy. But the obstinacy with which he sticks to that expression alone which his critics taught him, is only fresh evidence of both his confusion of mind and unfamiliarity with the subject.

* * *

Having pointed out by quotations from Kant that the expression "space is *Anschauung*" is as legitimately Kantian as the other phrase that it is "a form of *Anschauung*," I shall now proceed to explain why the quotation which Mr. Spencer makes from my article, although the eight words in quotation marks are literally quoted, is a misquotation. It is torn out of its context.

I did not blame the English translators of Kant at all, but I blamed his interpreters, among whom the English interpreters (not all English interpreters, but certainly some of them) are the worst, for "mutilating Kant's best thoughts, so that this hero of progress appears as a stronghold of antiquated views"; and as an instance I called attention to the misconception of Kant's term *Anschauung*, saying:

> "How different is Kant's philosophy, for instance, if his position with reference to time and space is mistaken!" 'Time and Space are our *Anschauung*,' Kant says. But his English translators declare 'Kant maintained that space and time are intuitions.' What a difference it makes if intuition is interpreted in the sense applied to it by the English intuitionalist school instead of its being taken in the original meaning of the word *Anschauung*."

The word "intuition" which is used by English translators is not wrong in itself; but it is liable to be misinterpreted.

The word "intuition" implies something mysterious; the word *Anschauung* denotes that which is immediately perceived, simply, as it were, by looking at it. So especially the sense-perceptions of the things before us are *Anschauungen*. There is absolutely nothing mysterious about *Anschauung*.

Mr. Spencer, believing that he had caught me in making unawares a blunder, tears the passage out of its context, ignores its purport, makes a point of an antithesis which had nothing in the world to do with the topic under discussion, only to throw on me the opprobrium of incompetence. Even if Mr. Spencer's antithesis of "intuition" and "forms of intuition" were of any consequence (as, unfortunately for Mr. Spencer, it is not), it would count for nothing against me because I did not speak of "forms" in the passage referred to, I simply alluded to one misinterpretation of the term *Anschauung* which is quite common among English Kantians. It was not required by the purpose

I had in view, to enter into any details as to what kind of *Anschauung* I meant, and an allusion to "form" or to any other subject would have served only to confound the idea which I intended to set forth in the paragraph from which Mr. Spencer quotes.

Misquotation of this kind, into which Mr. Spencer was inveigled by a hasty reading, should be avoided with utmost care, for it involves an insinuation. It leads away from the main point under discussion to side issues, and it misrepresents the author from whom the quotation is made. It insinuates a meaning which the passage does not bear and which was not even thought of in the context out of which it is torn.

Mr. Spencer quotes the passage as if I had preferred the term "intuition" to the term "form of intuition," or at least, as if I had no idea that Kant conceives Time and Space as "forms." Yet Mr. Spencer in trying to make out a point against me betrays his own lack of information. Kant insisted most emphatically on calling the forms of our sensibility (i. e. space and time) "*Anschauungen.*"

But Mr. Spencer's case is worse still. While he insists upon the statement that according to the translators of Kant space and time are "forms of intuition," which is at least correct, he uses twice in the very same paragraph the expression that according to Kant "space and time are forms of thought," which is incorrect. The forms of thought according to Kantian terminology are not space and time but the domain of the transcendental logic. Any one who confounds the two terms "forms of intuition" and "forms of thought" proves himself unable to form a correct opinion on Kant's philosophy. That is just characteristic of Kant that he regards time and space not as thought, nor as forms of thought, but as *Anschauungen* and in contradistinction to sense-intuitions (i. e. sensations) he calls them *reine Anschauungen* or *Formen der Anschauung.**

V.

Mr. Spencer commenting upon his criticism of Kant's idea of a Good Will, says:

"I find that in the above three paragraphs I have done Kant less than justice and more than justice—less, in assuming that his evolutionary view was limited to the genesis of our sidereal system, and more, in assuming that he had not contradicted himself.

"Clearly, I am indebted to Dr. Carus for enabling me to prove that Kant's defence of his theory of 'a good will' is, by his own showing, baseless."

Kant's idea of a good will has nothing to do with evolution, and we can abstain here from discussing whether or not Kant was an evolutionist. Whether evolution is true or not, what difference does it make to the proposition, that a good will is the only thing which can be called good without further qualification (*ohne Einschränkung*)? Pleasure is good, but is not absolutely good, there are cases in which pleasure is a very bad thing. We must qualify our statement and limit it to special cases. A good will, however, says Kant, is in itself good under all circumstances.

Mr. Spencer's arguments and the logical syllogisms which are peculiarly his own, are a severe tax on the patience of the most charitable reader.

Did Mr. Spencer prove the baselessness of Kant's proposition by proving evolution? Is it inconsistent to believe in evolution and at the same time to regard

*This is the only point which Mr. Spencer answers in his letter, on page 101, admitting the mistake and saying that it "was simply an inadvertence.", But it is an inadvertence with aggravating circumstances, furnishing an additional evidence of the fact that Mr. Spencer talks at random.

a good will as absolutely good, as good without reserve or limitation? I think not!

VI.

Mr. Spencer in admitting that "the general drift of the passages quoted makes it tolerably clear that Kant must have believed in the operation of natural causes . . . . in producing organic forms," adds:

> "He does not, however, extend the theory of natural genesis to exclusion of the theory of supernatural genesis."

How does Mr. Spencer prove his statement? Does he quote a passage from Kant which expresses his belief in supernaturalism? No, Mr. Spencer does not quote Kant, and it would be difficult to find a passage to suit that purpose. Mr. Spencer adduces a few unmeaning phrases gleaned at random and torn out of their context, and from these phrases he concludes that Kant believed in the supernatural. Kant spoke somewhere of "the wisdom of nature" who has things so arranged that the species might be preserved. If the wisdom of nature in preserving the species is to be taken literally, the phrase might prove that Kant believed nature to be a wise old woman. Kant spoke further of "the germ of reason placed in man whereby he is destined to social intercourse." Does the usage of the word "destined" really "imply divine intervention?" Mr. Spencer adds:

> "And this [viz. Kant's usage of these phrases] shows that I was justified in ascribing to him the belief that Space and Time, as forms of thought [sic!], are supernatural endowments."

What might we not prove by this kind of loose argumentation! Mr. Spencer should sweep before his own door ere he complains of Kant's abnormal reasoning.

Kant did not introduce any supernatural explauations; on the contrary, he proposed to exclude "supernatural genesis." He says e. g. in a passage of the "Critique of Judgment" quoted on page 39:

> "If we assume occasionalism for the production of organised beings, nature is thereby wholly discarded . . . . therefore it cannot be supposed that this system is accepted by any one who has had to do with philosophy."

And furthermore Kant rejects the partial admission of the supernatural, saying:

> "As though it were not the same to make the required forms arise in a supernatural manner at the beginning of the world as during its progress."

Mr. Spencer charges Kant with inconsistency. We do not intend to say that Kant was in all the phases of his development consistent with himself. But we do say that the charge of Mr. Spencer against Kant consists in this: the real Kant had said things which are incompatible with Mr. Spencer's view of Kant.

This settles the sixth point.

VII.

Mr. Spencer's reply to my criticism is a very strange piece of controversy and I have actually been at a loss, how to account for it.

The situation can be explained only by assuming that Mr. Spencer, being an impatient reader, when finding out that he disagreed with my propositions, could go no further and wrote his reply to me without having read my articles. This is very hard on a critic who, carefully avoiding everything that might look like fault-finding, is painstakingly careful in giving to the author criticised every means of investigating the truth himself and helps him in a friendly way to correct his errors.

There is only one consolation for me, which is, that I am in good company. The great thinker of Koenigsberg is very severely censured in almost all of Mr. Spencer's writings for ideas which he never held. And now Mr. Spencer confesses openly and with ingenuous sincerity, that his knowledge of Kant's writings is extremely limited. But why he condemns a man of whom he knows so little Mr. Spencer does not tell us.

Mr. Spencer says:

"My knowledge of Kant's writings is extremely limited. In 1844 a translation of his 'Critique of Pure Reason' (then I think lately published) fell into my hands, and I read the first few pages enunciating his doctrine of Time and Space; my peremptory rejection of which caused me to lay the book down.

"Twice since then the same thing has happened; for, being an impatient reader, when I disagree with the cardinal propositions of a work I can go no further.

"One other thing I knew. By indirect references I was made aware that Kant had propounded the idea that celestial bodies have been formed by the aggregation of diffused matter. Beyond this my knowledge of his conceptions did not extend; and my supposition that his evolutionary conception had stopped short with the genesis of sun, stars, and planets was due to the fact that his doctrine of Time and Space, as forms of thought [sic] anteceding experience, implied a supernatural origin inconsistent with the hypothesis of natural genesis."

Kant has been a leader in thought for the last century. It is very important to criticise his ideas wherever they are wrong, but his errors cannot be conquered by *ex cathedra* denunciations.

Darwin's habits in investigating and weighing the pros and cons of a question were very different from Mr. Spencer's, and Darwin's success is in no small degree due to the sternness with which he adhered to certain rules of reading and studying. We find in his

"Autobiography" certain reminiscences labelled "important" from which the following is instructive :

"I had also, during many years, followed a golden rule, namely, that whenever a published fact, a new observation or a thought, came across me, which was opposed to my general results, to make a memorandum of it without fail, for I had found by experience that such facts and thoughts were far more apt to escape from the memory than favorable ones."

Experience teaches that we can learn most from those authors with whom we do not agree. The ethics of reading and studying demand other habits than laying a book down when we disagree with its cardinal propositions. Such habits prevent progress and create prejudices.

* * *

Mr. Speecer has not answered my criticism at all. Mr. Spencer did not even take into consideration the passages quoted from Kant. He republished all the false statements of Kant's views, so inconsiderately made, together with all the perverse opinions based upon them. The assurance with which Mr. Spencer makes statements which have no foundation whatever is really perplexing even to a man who is well informed on the subject, and it will go far to convince the unwary reader.* What, however, shall become of the general tenor of philosophical criticism and controversy if a man of Mr. Spencer's reputation is so indifferent about being informed concerning the exact views of his adversary, if he is so careless in presenting them, if he makes positively erroneous statements on confessedly mere "supposition," and finally, if in consequence thereof he is flagrantly unjust in censuring errors which arise only from his own too prolific imagination ?

*The late Henry George called Mr. Spencer "the perplexed philosopher.'

We feel confident that Mr. Spencer will explain his side of the question satisfactorily. His mistakes being undeniable, we do not believe that he will seek to deny them. Yet we trust that Mr. Spencer as soon as he finds himself at fault, will not even make an attempt at palliation, that he will not blink the frank aknowledgment of his misstatements and also of having treated Kant with injustice. A man who has devoted his life to the search for truth will not suffer any blot to remain on his escutcheon.

[I abstain from altering the last paragraph which seems now out of date and will add only by way of Postscript my regret that Mr. Spencer has failed to fulfil my expectations. The only answer he ever made is the letter which is reproduced as the end of this discussion. I have been tardy in the republication of these criticisms, perhaps too tardy, but I still hoped that Mr. Spencer would by and by understand the situation and by a frank confession of his mistakes relieve me of the unpleasant task of repeating my charges and of having them appear in book form. I have come to the conclusion that for the sake of truth, of justice, and in the interest of the growing generation they should become more accessible to the reading public.]

A LETTER FROM MR. HERBERT SPENCER.

As I feel it a duty to reserve, for other purposes, the very small power of work now left to me, I am obliged to decline entering upon a controversy. I must leave readers to examine for themselves—little hoping, however, that they will do so.

One point only I wish to note. The use of the expression "forms of thought," instead of "forms of intuition," was simply an inadvertence;* as will be manifest on observing that though I have used the wrong expression in the note, I have used the right expression in the text (p. 203), as also throughout my criticism of Kant's doctrine in *The Principles of Psychology*, Part VII, Chapter IV, "The Reasonings of Metaphysicians," § 399. HERBERT SPENCER.

*This subject is discussed on pp. 83-86 and 95-96 of the present booklet.

INDEX.